LECTURES

ON THE

EPISTLE TO THE PHILIPPIANS.

LECTURES

ON

ST PAUL'S EPISTLE TO THE PHILIPPIANS.

BY

C. J. VAUGHAN, D.D.

DEAN OF LLANDAFF AND MASTER OF THE TEMPLE

FOURTH EDITION.

WIPF & STOCK · Eugene, Oregon

Wipf and Stock Publishers
199 W 8th Ave, Suite 3
Eugene, OR 97401

Lectures on St. Paul's Epistle to the Philippians, Fourth Edition
By Vaughan, C. J.
Softcover ISBN-13: 978-1-6667-3415-7
Hardcover ISBN-13: 978-1-6667-2970-2
eBook ISBN-13: 978-1-6667-2971-9
Publication date 8/18/2021
Previously published by Macmillan and Co., 1882

This edition is a scanned facsimile of
the original edition published in 1882.

PREFACE.

THESE Lectures, delivered in the Parish Church of Doncaster, are framed on the plan of a series of Expository Sermons preached in London in the year 1860, and afterwards published under the title of *Epiphany, Lent, and Easter*.

Each Lecture is prefaced by a literal translation from the original Greek[1] of the paragraph which forms its subject.

In these translations no attempt has been made to adhere to the words of the Authorized English Version. It is not more the right than I believe it to be the duty of every Christian Teacher to assist his Congregation, according to his ability, in drinking not of the stream only but at the spring of revealed

---

[1] The text employed, almost without exception, is that of Tischendorf's 2nd Edition, Leipsic, 1849.

Truth; to bring to bear upon the elucidation of Holy Scripture any gifts of discernment and knowledge with which it has pleased God to endow him; and while he respects the Authorized Version for its general correctness, and reveres it for its sacred associations, to endeavour to stir it into new activity by every appliance which may add energy to its language or precision to its sense.

Such endeavours imply no disparagement of the English Bible as the daily guide and companion of English Christians. No one will imagine that the bald and stiff translations prefixed to these Lectures are offered as substitutes for the graceful and idiomatic sentences which correspond to them in the Authorized Version. To supplement is not to supersede. And the more carefully our Congregations are instructed in the true meaning, the literal language, of the original Word of Inspiration, the less need will there be for a reconstruction of its popular form. For my own part I believe that the advantages of such a reconstruction would be far outweighed by its evils. Beyond the removal of a few obsolete terms, and the correction of a few acknowledged inaccuracies, any formal revision of the national Version would infallibly spoil more than it could improve. The

English Bible is a standard of taste, a model of language, a specimen of dignified simplicity. More than this, it is the heirloom of all families, and the link between successive generations of the faithful. It is easy to detect its blemishes: but where is the hand to which we would entrust its reformation?

The object of this publication will have been answered if it sends any one back to his Bible with more pleasure and with more intelligence; if it makes the particular Epistle of which it treats more full for him of meaning and of suggestion. It will shortly be followed by a like though longer work upon the Revelation of St John. And, if life be spared, other Books of Holy Scripture may be similarly illustrated in their turn.

Each Lecture contains first a somewhat minute explanation of the passage on which it is based, and then a practical application of the verse or clause selected as its text. It will be readily seen that that application has had special reference to the wants of the particular Congregation to which it was addressed. In some cases it might be questioned whether the directness of the appeal did not almost unfit it for a more extended circulation. But it may at least serve the purpose of shewing that the closest investigation of the language and argument of the Divine Word is no impediment to its employment for the higher purposes *of doctrine, of reproof, of correction, of instruction in righteousness.*

BAMBOROUGH,
October 11, 1862.

CONTENTS.

LECTURE I.

CHAP. I. 3. I thank my God upon every remembrance of you . 3

LECTURE II.

CHAP I. 6. Being confident of this very thing, that He which hath begun a good work in you will perform it until the day of Jesus Christ. 21

LECTURE III.

CHAP. I. 20. Christ shall be magnified in my body. . . . 39

LECTURE IV.

CHAP. I. 21. To me to live is Christ, and to die is gain. . . 55

LECTURE V.

CHAP I. 27. Only let your conversation be as it becometh the Gospel of Christ. 71

LECTURE VI.

Chap II 2. Fulfil ye my joy, that ye be likeminded. . . 85

LECTURE VII.

Chap II 10 That at the name of Jesus every knee should bow. 101

LECTURE VIII.

Chap II 12, 13 Work out your own salvation with fear and trembling . for it is God which worketh in you. . 117

LECTURE IX.

Chap II 16 Holding forth the word of life 133

LECTURE X.

Chap II 20. I have no man likeminded. 149

LECTURE XI.

Chap II. 27. He was sick, nigh unto death : but God had mercy on him 165

LECTURE XII.

Chap III 7 What things were gain to me, those I counted loss for Christ 181

LECTURE XIII.

CHAP. III. 8, 9. That I may win Christ, and be found in Him. 197

LECTURE XIV.

CHAP III. 10. That I may know Him, and the power of His resurrection. 213

LECTURE XV.

CHAP. III. 10 That I may know Him and the fellowship of His sufferings. 229

LECTURE XVI

CHAP. III. 13. Forgetting those things which are behind, and reaching forth unto those things which are before . 247

LECTURE XVII.

CHAP. III. 19, 20. Who mind earthly things. For our conversation is in heaven. 263

LECTURE XVIII.

CHAP. IV 5, 6. The Lord is at hand Be careful for nothing . 279

LECTURE XIX.

CHAP. IV. 8. Finally, brethren, whatsoever things are true, whatsoever things are honest, whatsoever things are just, whatsoever things are pure, whatsoever things are lovely, whatsoever things are of good report, if there be any virtue, and if there be any praise, think on these things. 295

LECTURE XX.

PAGE

CHAP. IV. 13 I can do all things through Christ which strengtheneth me 311

LECTURE XXI.

CHAP. IV 17. I desired fruit that may abound to your account . 327

LECTURE I.

PHILIPPIANS I. 1—11.

1 *PAUL and Timotheus, servants of Christ Jesus, to all the saints in Christ Jesus who are in Philippi, with bishops and*
2 *deacons: Grace to you, and peace, from God our Father and from the Lord Jesus Christ*
3, 4 *I thank my God for all my recollection of you, always in every prayer of mine making that supplication for you all*
5 *with joy, for your fellowship unto the Gospel from the first*
6 *day until now, being confident of this very thing, that He who began in you a good work will complete it until the day*
7 *of Jesus Christ, even as it is just for me to be thus minded in behalf of you all, because I have you in my heart (as) being all of you, both in my bonds and in the defence and*
8 *confirmation of the Gospel, my partners in the grace. For God is my witness, how I long after you all in the tender*
9 *mercies of Christ Jesus. And this I pray, that your love may yet more and more abound in further knowledge and*
10 *all perception, unto your testing things that differ, that ye may be pure and stedfast unto the day of Christ, complete*
11 *in the fruit of righteousness which is by means of Jesus Christ, unto the glory and praise of God.*

LECTURE I.

PHILIPPIANS I. 3.

I thank my God upon every remembrance of you

IT happens that the passage from which the text is taken is read twice in the Services of this day. It is read as the Epistle: it is read again as the second Lesson for this evening. I purpose to make it our subject on both these occasions: speaking this morning upon the passage generally, and selecting in the evening one verse full of reflections salutary for us both individually and as a congregation. It is probable that our attention may be directed for some following Sunday mornings to this Epistle of St Paul, while I hope to be enabled next Sunday evening to recommence the exposition of the Revelation of St John. May God prosper every undertaking by which, through this or that portion of His Holy Word, we seek to make Him better known on earth, better loved, and better served!

The Epistle to the Philippians has many points of peculiar interest for us.

The Church to which it is addressed was the first planted in Europe by St Paul's ministry. The 16th chapter of the Acts of the Apostles gives us the account of its foundation. St Paul had received a special summons into Macedonia. At Troas, on the extreme margin of Asia, he had seen in the night a vision of a Macedonian standing and praying him, saying, *Come over into Macedonia, and help us*[1]. He recognized in this vision an intimation of the will of God That Holy Spirit under whose guidance all his works for God, all his journeyings[2] and all his ministrations, were constantly performed, had evidently taken this means of directing his steps towards that western world of which we ourselves are inmates. He obeyed the call. He immediately sailed from Troas[3], and touching at the island of Samothrace in his course, reached the shores of Macedonia at Neapolis, and from thence passed rapidly to Philippi.

Again, we have the interest of knowing (it is probable) some of the very persons to whom this letter was written Not much more than ten years had elapsed between the foundation of the Philippian Church and its receipt of this letter. It might well be that amongst the recipients of St Paul's loving counsels in writing, were many of those to whom at

[1] Acts xvi 9 [2] Acts xvi. 6, 7. [3] Acts xvi. 11, 12.

the beginning he had spoken the Gospel amidst circumstances of great distress and of great joy Lydia[1], the first of his converts in that city—Lydia, whose heart the Lord had opened to attend to the things spoken by Paul; the poor maiden[2], whom at the same season he had delivered from the possession of an evil spirit; and the jailer[3], whose remarkable conversion has been a topic of peculiar interest to Christians in all times, and one which we ourselves have recently dwelt upon, not, I would hope, without a blessing; these persons may have been amongst those who gathered together—perhaps in the very house[4] of Lydia herself—to hear the message of God as sent to them in the familiar hand of their beloved Apostle and Evangelist.

And he, the Apostle to whom under God they owed the knowledge of the Gospel, what had happened to him since he first left Philippi? and where and in what circumstances was he now? He had gone from Philippi to Thessalonica, to Berea, to Athens, to Corinth, to Ephesus, to Jerusalem[5] From thence he had gone through Galatia and Phrygia to Ephesus, remaining there on this occasion from two to three years[6]. On his departure from

---

[1] Acts xvi 14, 15. [2] Acts xvi. 16—18 [3] Acts xvi. 27—34
[4] Acts xvi 15, 40; compare Rom xvi 5, 1 Cor xvi 19, Col iv. 15, Philem. 2. [5] Acts xvii. 1, 10, 15; xviii. 1, 19, 22.
[6] Acts xviii. 23; xix. 1, 10, 22; compare xx. 31.

Ephesus[1] he had again made the tour of Macedonia, and doubtless had not left Philippi unvisited. The first visit having been about A D 52, the second would probably fall within the year 57 After spending three months in Greece, he again made Philippi his starting-point for Asia[2]. We track his course from Philippi to Troas, to Mitylene, to Miletus: there (at Miletus[3]) he addresses the elders of the Church of Ephesus, summoned thither to avoid the delay of a special visit to a place at some distance from the coast Thence he completes his voyage to the Holy Land, and reaches Jerusalem[4] And there he becomes a prisoner[5]. Rescued from the violence of his Jewish countrymen by the strong arm of the Roman power, he remains for some time at the head-quarters of the Roman government in Judæa, the seaport town of Cæsarea[6], where he is called upon more than once to defend himself before rulers and kings[7]; and at last he begins that voyage to Rome of which we have a minute and graphic account in the 27th chapter of the Acts, and of which we read the completion, after delay, danger, and shipwreck, in the 28th chapter. The sacred history leaves him at Rome[8], awaiting his hearing before the Emperor, in

---

[1] Acts xx 1, 2.
[2] Acts xx. 3, 6.
[3] Acts xx. 6, 14, 15, 17.
[4] Acts xxi. 1—15.
[5] Acts xxi. 33.
[6] Acts xxiii. 23, xxiv 27.
[7] Acts xxiv. 1; xxv. 6; xxvi. 1.
[8] Acts xxviii. 30, 31.

circumstances of considerable advantage for prosecuting his work as *an ambassador of Christ in bonds*[1]. And from thence, it cannot be doubted, the Epistle to the Philippians was written during his detention[2]. We shall probably not err in fixing the date of the letter towards the end rather than the beginning of that imprisonment which the history in the Acts tells us lasted through two whole years, and in the course of which, though probably at an earlier part in it, the Epistles to the Ephesians, to the Colossians, and to Philemon, were written also The year A.D. 63 may be regarded as the date of the letter.

Now in what manner does he address this congregation of ten or eleven years' standing in the faith? There is a great distinctness, a great individuality, in the tone and style of his description and of his exhortation. It is quite unlike that in which he writes to the Romans, the Corinthians, the Galatians, or the Ephesians. It is quite evident that he feels towards this congregation a very peculiar affection. They had been singularly thoughtful, singularly affectionate towards him. Again and again, he reminds them, they had sent contributions for his support[3]. The present letter seems to have been occasioned by an offering of this nature[4]. And however well disciplined in the school of suffering, however long and thoroughly

---

[1] Eph vi. 20.
[2] Phil. i. 13; iv. 22.
[3] Phil. iv. 15.
[4] Phil iv. 14, 18.

instructed in the great Christian science of *knowing how to be abased and how to abound*, of knowing how *in whatsoever state he was therewith to be content*[1]; he had not failed to learn also another great Christian lesson, of thankfulness to God for every blessing, and under God to all those who are instrumental in bestowing each

And now I will ask you to look with me into the first paragraph of the Epistle itself. It extends from the first to the 11th verse. All save the first two verses are included in the Epistle for this day.

Paul and Timotheus, servants of Christ Jesus, to all the saints in Christ Jesus who are in Philippi[2]. Timotheus and Silas also had been with St Paul when he first preached at Philippi[3]. Timotheus (but not Silas) had been with him also on his third visit there, of which we have the record in the 20th chapter of the Acts[4]. And Timotheus (but not Silas) was now with him during his imprisonment at Rome[5]. They are described together, Paul and Timotheus, by a title common to them both; that title which is at once the humblest and the noblest of all; as *servants*, or *slaves, of Christ Jesus*. They were not both Apostles, but even an Apostle is a servant too, and it is his highest honour to be thus designated; as one whose very will

---

[1] Phil. iv. 11, 12.   [2] *Verse* 1
[3] Acts xv. 40, xvi 3, 19; xvii 14   [4] Acts xx 4.
[5] Phil. i. 1, Col. i 1; Philem. 1

is merged and lost in that of his Master, his Saviour, his Lord and his God.

To all the saints in Christ Jesus. A *saint* is a *consecrated* person, one who is set apart by God Himself for His special worship and service. It does not refer so much to the individual character, to the peculiar Christian attainments of the person; but rather to the separation and consecration which God has bestowed in his call by the Gospel, and in his admission into the Church of Christ by Baptism and by the gift of the Holy Spirit. Such a person is a *saint in Christ Jesus.* He is admitted into union with Christ: he is included in Christ: he is a part of the body of Christ[1]: let him see that he lives and walks as such!

With bishops and deacons. The Philippians are reminded at the very outset, that God is not the author of confusion, but of order, in the churches of His saints[2]. All are not ministers, though all are members, of the Church of Christ. Let those who form the congregation duly recognize and receive the ministrations of those who are set over them in the Lord[3]. Let them not forget discipline in privilege If they are Christians, they have still something to learn: they need pastors and teachers, even though they have but one Lord and one Master.

---

[1] Rom. vii. 4; 1 Cor. xii. 27, Gal. iii. 27. [2] 1 Cor. xiv. 33
[3] 1 Thess v. 12, 13.

Bishops and deacons. While the Apostles were upon earth, they were what we should call the Bishops of the Church . the bishops here spoken of are rather the elders, the presbyters, the pastors, of the congregation. It is the same word rendered in the 20th chapter of the Acts *overseers*, and used there as synonymous with *elders* or *presbyters*[1]. *He sent to Ephesus and called the elders of the church* And then he says to these elders, *Take heed therefore to yourselves, and to all the flock over the which the Holy Ghost hath made you overseers*, or *bishops*[2].

Grace, free favour, *be to you, and peace*, in the sense of that favour, *from God our Father, and the Lord Jesus Christ*[3].

I thank my God upon every remembrance of you; or more exactly, *for all my recollection of you*[4]. Everything which I remember about you makes me thank my God for you. *My God.* God, who is the God of all, is the God also of each. Though a Christian is not to be selfish, is not to forget that God is the God of all men, and (in a special sense) of all Christians, yet he is to remember also that he personally, he individually, stands in a particular relation to that God of all. He may say *My God*, and feel that there is a meaning in that appropriation, just as in another place he is taught to say not *My Father*, but *Our Father*, and

[1] Acts xx. 17.
[2] Acts xx 28.
[3] *Verse* 2.
[4] *Verse* 3.

to remember that what God is to him He is to others besides him.

Always in every supplication of mine making that supplication for you all with joy[1]. He never prays without remembering them. And that remembrance is always a joyful remembrance . for the reason which follows.

For (on the ground of) your fellowship in the Gospel —more exactly, *your fellowship unto*, or *in the service of, the Gospel—from the first day* that you became Christians *until now*[2]*:* that is, remembering how you have always felt and shewn your interest in the Gospel by personal devotion of life, and by a constant readiness to promote its welfare and success.

Being confident of this very thing, that He who began in you a good work will complete it[3], will bring it to its due accomplishment, will bring first one and then another of you to a safe and blessed end, in your individual sanctification and salvation, *until the day of Jesus Christ: even as it is just*, meet and right, *for me to be thus minded in behalf of you all, because I have you in my heart*, as *being all of you, both in my bonds and in the defence and confirmation of the Gospel, my partners in the grace*[4]. I cannot but feel this confidence that God will perfect His work in you, because I see in you those who are my companions in tribulation, fellow-

[1] *Verse* 4.
[2] *Verse* 5.
[3] *Verse* 6
[4] *Verse* 7.

sufferers with me in the cause of the Gospel, and who are thus proved to be, in deed and in truth, partners with me in the grace and favour of God.

For God is my witness how I long after you all in the tender mercies of Christ Jesus[1]. I can appeal to God Himself as to the sincerity of my concern for you, of my longing and yearning after you in absence, in the exercise of that compassionate love which was first in Christ Jesus.

And this I pray, that your love may yet more and more abound in further knowledge[2]. The word expresses *fuller and deeper knowledge;* not the first acquaintance with a subject, but the more intimate and profound entrance into it which comes from long and diligent study. *And in all perception.* The last word is connected (in the original language) with that found in the 5th chapter of the Epistle to the Hebrews: *But strong meat,* solid food, *belongs to them that are of full age, even to them who by reason of use* (habit) *have their senses exercised to discern between good and evil*[3]. The *perception* here spoken of is properly a perception by the senses; a discrimination which is the result of long habit; the sort of discernment of the properties of things that differ (as the next verse expresses it) which comes with practice and experience, and which in moral matters may almost be described as the acquisition of a new sense, not less potent in

[1] *Verse* 8.   [2] *Verse* 9.   [3] Heb. v. 14.

its own department, than the sense of touch, smell, or taste, in things bodily and material. This is St Paul's prayer for the Philippians: an increase of discernment and discrimination in matters of duty.

That ye may approve things that are excellent; or as the margin gives it, *that ye may try things that differ*[1]; that ye may put to the test things which differ in their moral quality, and as a consequence of this examination, may approve those which stand the test, those which, when tested and sifted on Christian principles, are found to be altogether right and good. *That so ye may be pure and stedfast unto the day of Christ Pure;* that is, genuine, unadulterated, without admixture of debasing ingredients and *stedfast;* properly, *not stumbling;* and so, stable, upright, constant. And the whole expression may remind us of the concluding words of the Epistle of St Jude: *Now unto Him that is able to keep you from falling,* or more exactly, *from stumbling, and to present you faultless before the presence of His glory with exceeding joy,* &c[2] *Pure and stedfast unto the day of Christ: complete in (fulfilled or completed as to) the fruit of righteousness which is by means of Jesus Christ, unto the glory and praise of God.* It is only by the help of Jesus Christ that we can bear any fruit: as He says Himself, *As the branch cannot bear fruit of itself, except it abide in the vine; no more can ye, except ye abide in me*[3]. *The fruit of*

[1] *Verse* 10.   [2] Jude 24, 25.   [3] John xv. 4.

righteousness is all *by Jesus Christ.* That is one thought. The other is, that, where and when that fruit is manifested, it is all *to the glory and praise of God.* There is no possibility of separating Christ from God. Whatever Christ does, God does: whatever Christ enables His servants to be or to do, all redounds to God's glory. *I and my Father are one*[1].

And now, reserving (as I have said) a single verse for separate consideration this evening, I wish to draw from the general aspect of this passage one concluding remark. It is, as to the feeling which ought to subsist between a minister and his congregation; more especially, how he ought to be able to think of them, and what he ought to make his special prayer for them, whenever in the Providence of God he is for a time separated from them.

St Paul was able to thank God in his compulsory detention at Rome, for all that he remembered of his beloved Church at Philippi. Whenever he prayed, he was able to make his prayer for them with joy. He could think of them—to go no further than the few verses now before us—as earnestly and resolutely set upon practising and upon helping the Gospel. They did not shrink even from suffering for it. My brethren, if St Paul had been writing to us, could he have thus expressed himself? Could he have said with regard to the great bulk of this congregation, that in

[1] John x. 30

their several stations, at their various ages, according to their different gifts and talents, they were truly loving and living the Gospel? Let each one ask himself, Could he have said this of me?

One thing St Paul was able to say, alike for himself and for them; that there was the strongest possible tie between them of mutual love. And surely to be able to say this is no small matter. Surely where a minister and his congregation love each other fervently, there must be something of Christ in that feeling and in that place. God grant that this may be more and more true with regard to us! Let it be always a pain to us to be parted. Let our thoughts be always with each other in absence. Let it always be an unfeigned joy to us to be reunited in body as in spirit. One year has quickly flown by since that important relation was first established between us, the issues of which are only to be realized in the Judgment. Greater kindness, surely, was never received by any ministers from those whom they would seek to serve: may they more and more zealously repay it in devotion of life as in affection of heart!

St Paul loved and was loved by these Philippians; and he shewed and returned it by his prayers for them. He recognized and valued their affection: he felt that their love for him sprang out of love to Christ, and shewed itself in an active and diffusive charity. But he knew also that it is not safe in this world to rest in that which is: while we stay here, we must always be moving onwards. And what he desired for them was, that their love might abound yet more and more in a deeper knowledge and in a more experienced judgment. He would have them dig deeper into the treasures of Divine truth. He would have them grow in the knowledge of God and of His Son Jesus Christ He would have them feel more seriously that eternal life itself must begin here below; and that this is life eternal, that a man may know God, as alone He can be known, in His Son, and by His Spirit[1]. My brethren, there is room amongst us also, I am quite sure, for this prayer and for this exhortation. However kindly affectioned we may be to those who are over us or to those who are around us in the Lord; however ready to respond to the call of charity, when it bids us feed the hungry, visit the sick, or feel for the sorrowful; I am persuaded that we have much yet to learn from the stores of Divine Revelation, much yet to learn from close personal communion with that God and that Saviour whom the Word of Inspiration makes known to us. A truly religious, a truly Christian life, consists, for us, in that which is so briefly and so beautifully expressed in Scripture as *walking with God*[2]. Which of us all does that? Which of us all really sets God always before him[3], and whether he

[1] John xvii 3.   [2] Gen. v. 24.   [3] Psalm xvi. 8.

eats or drinks, or whatsoever he does, does all to His glory[1]? The very sound of the words is reproving. They do not at all describe the life of most of us We take little trouble to know God better than we do, or to bring the thought of Him into our daily life And therefore it is that we can so little enter into the feeling of those who have longed through life, with yearnings not to be repressed and not to be uttered, for the coming of that day when their eyes should actually *see the King in His beauty*, and *behold the land that is very far off* [2].

Nor less do we need the prayer that we may increase in judgment, and approve the things that are excellent. How few are there upon earth—how few certainly amongst us—who have by long use their senses exercised to discern good and evil! How few who by long intercourse with the All-wise and the All-holy have acquired that spiritual insight and that spiritual instinct which makes them, in the difficult decisions and at the ambiguous turning-points of life, infallibly refuse the evil and choose the good! We have known perhaps a few such men and such women in our time, a few persons—just one or two in a large family or in a wide acquaintance—to whom we could always apply for guidance and direction in the certainty that what they advised they would advise as those who had obtained mercy of the

[1] 1 Cor x 31. [2] Isaiah xxxiii. 17.

Lord to be faithful[1] How ought we to long and to pray that we ourselves, for ourselves and for others also, might be endowed with this great gift, called here by the name of judgment, or (more exactly) of perception! It comes, I would repeat it, only from being much with God, from being often in each day in His presence, *hidden privily*, as the Psalmist expresses it, *in His pavilion from the strife of tongues*[2], from the conflicts of selfishness, from the din of earth Practise this, my brethren, and depend upon it, the moments spent with God, on your knees before Him, with your windows fully opened[3] towards the Jerusalem above, will be of all the happiest and the most delightful—fruitful in the brightest memories, and preparatory for the most glorious future.

[1] 1 Cor. vii. 25.   [2] Psalm xxxi. 20   [3] Dan vi 10

TWENTY-SECOND SUNDAY AFTER TRINITY,
October 27, 1861.

LECTURE II.

[This Lecture, though devoted almost exclusively to topics of congregational and local interest, is retained in its place, as an indication of the intended bearing of the whole series upon practical life]

LECTURE II.

PHILIPPIANS I. 6

Being confident of this very thing, that He which hath begun a good work in you will perform it until the day of Jesus Christ.

THE day of *Jesus Christ.* Yes, that is the goal of our race. That is the point to which every Christian eye is directed. Every other day of our lives, every other day of the world's existence, is a *day;* a common, ordinary, casual day, and no more: this is *the day*. It is sometimes so called in Scripture without further epithet or explanation. *Every man's work shall be made manifest; for* the day *shall declare it, because it shall be revealed in fire*[1]. *Not forsaking the assembling of ourselves together, as the manner of some is; but exhorting one another: and so much the more as ye see* the day *approaching*[2].

My brethren, is this our estimate of the day of

[1] 1 Cor. iii. 13.   [2] Heb. x 25.

Jesus Christ? Do we remember, do we live in the remembrance of, all that is involved in it? *The day of Jesus Christ* is the day which belongs to Him; the day which is His altogether; the day which shall reveal Him as He is, disclose His real greatness, put down every rival power, and erect His throne for ever as the *King of kings and Lord of lords*[1] Where shall we be then? Shall we be among those slothful and disobedient servants, *who shall be punished with everlasting destruction from the presence of the Lord*[2]? or rather among those who have been long waiting for Him with loins girt and lights burning[3], and to whom the day of the revelation of Jesus Christ will be also the day of their own final manifestation as the sons of God[4]?

Let these thoughts solemnize our minds for the work now before us. We are to meditate together on the words of St Paul, already introduced to you this morning, in which he expresses his confidence, with regard to a particular congregation and to the individuals of whom it was composed, that God who had begun a good work in them would carry it on and consummate it against that day of Jesus Christ which is to decide the destiny of every child of man. The words were written to a particular congregation: but you will see that there was nothing in them of a

[1] Rev. xix. 16.
[2] Matt. xxv. 26, 2 Thess i 9
[3] Luke xii. 35.
[4] Rom. viii. 19.

merely local or transitory import: they ought to be equally true of all congregations of professed Christians, they are equally true of all those who are personally Christians indeed, passing through the wilderness of this world towards the rest which remaineth for the people of God[1].

I purpose this evening, with all plainness, to point out to you some of the marks of that congregation, and of that individual, in which or in whom God has evidently begun a good work. And then we shall be able to press home the comfort, or else the serious warning, conveyed in the thought of the completion of that good work against the day of Jesus Christ

The words, *who hath begun a good work in you*, might be rendered, *who hath begun a good work among you*. And thus they are well capable of the two applications already proposed, an application to the congregation, and an application to the individual.

1. There is such a thing as a good work begun among a body of professed Christians. And as the subject is a wide one, we will confine ourselves to the thought, not so much of the general conduct, of the private life, of a Church like that of the Philippians of old, or like that of this Parish at the present day, but rather of what may be called its congregational life, its actual assemblies for worship, and its voluntary associations for purposes of charity; its aspect in short

[1] Heb. iv. 9.

before God and man, as a body gathered out of the world to set forth *the praises of Him who has called us out of darkness into His marvellous light*[1].

We can form some idea of the worship of the first Christians. The book of the Acts of the Apostles gives us some glimpses of it. I might refer you to the 4th chapter of that Book, or again to the 20th chapter, for striking examples of what worship may be, what praise may be, what prayer may be, what preaching may be, what communion may be, when men's minds are in earnest, when they truly believe what they profess to believe, when they have God's presence really with them, and when they are set upon *growing in grace and in the knowledge of their Lord and Saviour*[2]. It is then no reluctant gathering, and no listless, indolent, drowsy gathering: there is then no such thing as a half-empty building, no such thing as a singing or a responding by proxy; no complaint of the length of a Sermon or of the monotony of the prayers, no bringing of the world hither in our thoughts, and no returning hence to the world as with a glad and joyful rebound from an irksome stretch and strain of duty. God can hardly be said to have begun a good work in us as a congregation, where any one of these things is still prevalent, still characteristic.

Now I hope we are not unthankful for many signs of good amongst us in reference to our public worship.

---

[1] 1 Pet. ii 9. [2] 2 Pet. iii 18.

Not only have we a beautiful building to worship in, in exchange for those *upper rooms*[1] of private houses which sheltered or concealed the devotions of the primitive Church: not only have we admirable forms of worship; a Liturgy sound in doctrine, simple in language, and consecrated by the associations of many generations: we have also large assemblages of worshippers, order and propriety of demeanour in worship, and respectful attention during the reading and the preaching of God's Holy Word. These things are good, we ought to thank God for them: it might be very different; it often has been, or it is elsewhere even now, very different. But yet, my brethren, we must not rest in that which we have already attained. If there is some reason to hope that God has begun a good work among us, there is yet much which might almost make us doubt it. Not only must we remember that large numbers of persons—Christians still, many of them, in name and by Baptism—who go nowhere, even on the Lord's Day, to worship God; persons to be counted in this place, we fear, by hundreds and by thousands: not only is there this to humble us, when we are beginning to feel that God's work is visible and progressive in this place. there is much more, there is that which is nearer to us than this I will speak as I feel, using plain words that cannot be misunderstood.

[1] Acts 1 13; xx. 8

i   And first I will lament to you once again, as I have done at former times, the comparative scantiness of our congregations in the two earlier services of the Lord's Day. It is unmeaning to speak of this defect in addressing those who are assembled on those occasions, and who by the fact itself are shewn not to need the reproof. I will speak of it now in the Evening congregation, and enquire of you—many of whom, as we are well aware, attend the House of God only in the evening,—what becomes of you during the earlier hours of the Lord's Day? What is there to prevent you from beginning as well as ending the day with public prayer and praise? The Providence of God, striving with human neglect and ingratitude, has preserved to us in this land the ordinance of His day of rest: other nations have flung it away, have lost altogether its sacred character, and made it a day of more than common frivolity and dissipation. This is not yet quite our case as a nation. Then I ask, what use are we making of this great privilege—of this standing ordinance of a Divine humanity? Are we wasting its precious hours—those hours which are not one too many for the great object, of resting from our common work, not in torpor or lethargy, but in thankfulness and in communing with God—are we wasting these precious hours, their prime at least and their noonday, in a more than common indolence and dulness? Where is now that family, among the poor more especially, which comes forth from its door on the Sunday morning as a family—leaving but one, if one, behind—to hear of their Saviour's work, and to celebrate their Saviour's praise? These things are of the past. It is now thought much if even one or two of a family go anywhere—one to this Church, another to that Chapel —even they without concord or communion—the rest going nowhere, or going only to one of the devil's haunts and meeting-places And I can scarcely say that God has, in this sense, begun a good work in us as a congregation, until His house is filled three times in the day by persons eager to worship, and looking forward to it as the week's solace and refreshment

Is there, let me ask, any special hindrance in this place to the Morning attendance of the congregation? Is it the Saturday Market, involving late hours, late payments and late purchases, late rest and consequently late rising? If it be so, and if no limitations or modifications can be devised to correct the evil, I well know that those who here rule in such matters will not grudge the inconvenience which might arise from even changing the day of the Market. It is of more consequence that the Sunday should be sacred than that the Saturday should be busy. It is of more consequence that all should worship God than that the most convenient day should be found for buying and selling. The one is a matter of the soul and of eternity; the other is of the earth, earthly But let us take heed also lest in all this we be but framing excuses for our own idleness, excuses which the coming day of Jesus Christ will utterly discomfit and destroy.

ii. I will pass now from the attendance to the service And here, keeping before our minds the example of a primitive congregation, such as that to which St Paul wrote in the text, we shall have no difficulty in representing to ourselves what Church worship should be Church worship ought to be the union of a number of individual devotions. It ought to be the combined act of a multitude of persons, each separately interested and consciously concerned in every part of that which is done Prayers and praises, confessions, supplications and intercessions, psalms read or chanted, and hymns sung, the chapters here read, the sermons here preached, all ought to be the concern of all: there ought to be no flagging interest, no wandering or vacant look, and (in a considerable part of the service) no silent tongue In other places, near and far off, even a musical service is found to be no impediment to united worship. There have been those—ministers honoured in their generation—who have found their congregational music flat and lifeless, and have left it vigorous, animated, and inspiriting. I will humbly hope that it may be so with us. It cannot be effected without exertion; what indeed can, that is worth effecting? And it cannot be effected by a minister alone: his people must help him. I have thought it well thus publicly to ask your help, my beloved brethren, in infusing new life into our services I would request that during this coming week any persons—more especially any boys and young men, whether of a higher or a humbler class in life—who are capable of rendering the help of their voices to our Church music, will give me the pleasure of receiving their names as a voluntary addition to the strength of our choir. We will then make such arrangements as may be most convenient to them, for giving effect to their will to aid us. I am sure that they will never repent of having sought to turn to the benefit of the congregation a gift which God has given them.

It happened to me a month ago, to be present in a Church in one of the greatest of our northern towns, where it was impossible not to be struck with the beauty and heartiness of the music. The united voice of the congregation seemed to be giving utterance to God's praises; and the effect was indeed (to use the Scriptural figure) *as the sound of many waters*[1]. I found afterwards that, out of a large body of singing men and boys employed in that Church, there was not one who deigned to accept any payment: it would be the greatest of affronts, the minister said, to offer to any one of them any remuneration. Why might not

[1] Rev. xiv. 2, xix 6.

our own choir, I could not but ask myself, be largely supplemented from such voluntary aid? I trust and hope that no indolence and no false shame will be allowed by any one who now hears me to prevent him from giving himself, in this sense as in one still higher, to his Saviour's service. And let those who cannot do this, who cannot actually join themselves to the choir—and here I speak rather to the Christian women of the congregation—yet set it before themselves as a real and a high object, to make the services of this House of God as hearty and as vigorous as possible Let them utter His praises aloud with their lips, and sing them with their voice. Let them learn to do so, and also practise it Surely it is not too much to ask of those who value the opportunities of edification here enjoyed, that they qualify themselves to take part in the worship as it is here conducted. If indeed it is impossible to give to a musical service a congregational character, then that service itself must be wrong and ought to be replaced by one merely read Public worship must be the act of the congregation, or God is not honoured in it. But I am reluctant to believe that that which has been found possible and delightful in neighbouring towns, a congregational musical service, is a thing impossible here. Depend upon it, a want of interest, a want of zeal, is the cause, if it be so; and not a want of skill or a want of power. I earnestly hope, I fully believe, that a great change will come.

iii. And now, while I am still speaking of signs of good in a congregation, I would remind you that that season of the year is fast approaching, at which we must avail ourselves of lengthened evenings for affording to those whose education in earlier years has been defective, the opportunity of redeeming lost time, so far as it can be done, by diligent application now to the rudiments of knowledge Evening classes for men, and evening classes (in another place) for boys also, will shortly be formed And as we would invite those who have had few advantages, or have neglected their advantages, in early years, to seek earnestly the instruction which will thus be offered them ; so, on the other hand, we must again throw ourselves upon the kindness of the better educated, and especially of some of the young men, of this congregation, for help in teaching Last year that help was kindly and cheerfully given, at no small sacrifice of time and strength I know that it will not be denied us in the coming winter And in this matter also I would ask to be early informed upon whose aid we may reckon

If in two points already touched upon I have addressed my application necessarily to men, it is not because I am unaware of the special work of women in a Christian body, or because I am unthankful for what we have here experienced of its value. And let me say that there are two particular works of good in which at this time we are anxious to engage their service.

iv. The first of these is, a more watchful and individual oversight, out of school-hours, of those children who are under instruction in our Schools, more especially of the elder scholars in our Girls' School. If those who teach in our Sunday School would make it (more than they have ever yet done) a part of their business to visit the homes of their scholars, and thus, both personally and through their parents, to carry through the week the influence gained on the Sunday, they would in many cases, I am persuaded, save a young life from contamination and ruin, prevent much dangerous license, control many a wandering step, and give that timely individual warning for lack of which ignorance runs on into folly, folly into vice, and vice into ruin both of body and soul

v. The second suggestion is with reference to a particular office which has practically fallen into disuse among the poor of the flock, the office of Sponsors in Baptism In this place the custom appears to be not only that the parents are sponsors for their own children, but that they are in fact the only sponsors; the third sponsor being often some casual bystander, whose office towards the child begins and ends with the ceremony itself. Thus the intention of this rule of our Church is entirely frustrated: there is no additional guarantee for a Christian education, beyond what Nature herself has provided in the parent. if the parent be ungodly or vicious, if the parent be selfish and unfeeling, or if the parent be removed early by death, there is no Christian interest on which the child can fall back ; no one pledged before God and the Church to keep a friendly eye on that child's culture, bodily, mental, or spiritual ; he is to grow up as he may, the creature of accident, of circumstance, and of companionship Has it ever occurred to the Christian women of this congregation, how great a benefit they might confer upon the children of the poor by becoming sponsors for them ? If the District Visitors, for example, and if the Sunday School Teachers, and if a few others voluntarily offering themselves, would permit application to be made to them, one or another, in behalf of those who are about to be brought to the font of Baptism without any proper sponsors , if they would, in such cases, be present at the font, to join their prayers with those of the Minister and of the parents, and to give life and meaning to the service as they might do by their very presence , and if they would regard any child for whom they had thus answered, as possessing a claim upon their notice, upon their kindness, and upon their interest in his Christian training , I am persuaded that a new bond of spiritual brotherhood would be formed and cemented among the various ranks of our Parishioners· parents would shew, in most cases, to persons thus connected with their children, no slight respect and deference in their future management , and mercy in this as in all other instances would be found indeed to be *twice blessed*, blessing as much her that gives as them that receive. I need not say how thankfully we shall accept the names of those whose hearts may be inclined to respond to this call.

The words now spoken will not have been thrown away, if they should impress any persons here present with the feeling how wide a scope there is in a Parish and in a congregation for the exercise of various gifts and various energies in the service of Christ and of His Church You have been reminded to-night of no less than four distinct and definite kinds of agency in behalf of God's work amongst us. Surely it is good for any man to be called out of himself, out of his own little circle of selfish interests and personal pleasures, to do something, something real, however humble, in the service of others and in the cause of charity. We must not prescribe to any one what he shall do: we only ask him to see that he do something, not for himself, but for Christ's Church and for God's poor. Where this will shews itself, shews itself freely, and shews itself widely, there we may indeed say with truth that God has begun a good work in a congregation, and we may look forward with comfort and hope to its future consummation in souls rescued, blessed, and saved in the day of our Lord Jesus Christ.

2. The allotted time has been fully occupied in these collective thoughts, these suggestions which

concern not the individual, but the congregation. Yet we will not complain of this. Perhaps the subject which has occupied us may have more in it of what is personal, of what is humbling and of what is quickening to individuals, than is at first sight apparent. And at all events a brief concluding word may bring home the text strongly and decisively to ourselves.

Confident, St Paul says, *of this very thing, that He which hath begun a good work in you will perform it until the day of Jesus Christ.* In which of us, my brethren, has God begun this good work? We are not lost, any one of us, in a crowd. each one has his own state, his own life or else his own living death, in the sight of God who searcheth the heart Which of the two conditions is ours? Do we ask a sign? a test and touchstone of our condition? I might mention many: let one suffice. Who amongst us really prays? I do not ask, Who prays with comfort? or, Who prays with delight? or, Who prays with filial affiance and confidence? In seeking to decide the question whether God has begun His good work in one of us, I am satisfied to ask, Which of us really prays? Which of us, whether in light or in darkness —which of us, whether peacefully or anxiously—which of us, whether half in heaven, or amidst many doubts and much fear—which of us prays to God in his heart, in the name of Jesus Christ? O it is the living without God, the dispensing with God, the doing without Christ, the not either loving or fearing Him, which is the terrible, the black, the desperate state for a creature and for a sinner. He who prays—in other words, he who wants God, he who cries out for Christ, he who watches and waits *until the day break and the shadows flee away*[1], until *the Sun of righteousness shall arise* upon him *with healing in His wings*[2]—in that man, I will venture to say, God has begun His work of grace. Let him wait on, let him watch on, let him pray on, let him accept no substitute for Christ, no counterfeit of Christ; let him tell no lies to himself as to being what he is not or having what he has not, and in due time—I say not when—I say not how fully—for God gives no account to man of these matters[3]—but I say that at last—I say that in some measure—in death, if not in life—in eternity, if not in this world—God will lift up the light of His countenance upon him and give him peace[4] and thus the words will be verified in him, in all their force and in all their sweetness, *Being confident of this very thing, that He which hath begun a good work in you will perform it*—will present[5] you washed and justified and sanctified[6]—*in the day of Jesus Christ.*

[1] Cant ii 17 [2] Mal iv. 2. [3] Job xxxiii 13
[4] Numb. vi. 26, Ps. iv. 6 [5] 2 Cor. iv 14. [6] 1 Cor. vi 11

TWENTY-SECOND SUNDAY AFTER TRINITY,
October 27, 1861.

LECTURE III.

PHILIPPIANS I. 12—20.

12 *But I would ye should understand, brethren, that the things which concern me have come rather to the furtherance*
13 *of the Gospel, so that my bonds became manifest in Christ*
14 *in all the (Prætorian) camp and to all others, and that most of the brethren in the Lord, trusting to my bonds, are much*
15 *more bold to speak the word without fear   Some indeed even from a motive of envy and strife, and some also from a motive*
16 *of good will, proclaim Christ. the one from love*[1]*, knowing*
17 *that I am set for the defence of the Gospel; but the others from a factious spirit announce Christ, not purely, thinking*
18 *to stir up affliction for my bonds   For what* [*is it*]*?   Notwithstanding, every way, whether in pretence or in truth, Christ is announced; and in this I rejoice, yea, and will*
19 *rejoice. For I know that this will result to me in salvation through your supplication and the supply of the Spirit of*
20 *Jesus Christ, according to my earnest expectation and hope that in nothing I shall be ashamed, but that in all boldness, as always, so now also, Christ shall be magnified in my body, whether by means of life or by means of death.*

[1] The text here followed inverts the order of the Authorized Version in verses 16, 17

LECTURE III.

PHILIPPIANS I 20.

Christ shall be magnified in my body.

WE have heard of St Paul's feeling towards his beloved Church at Philippi in absence, and of his prayers for them, *that love might abound yet more and more in deeper knowledge and in a more discriminating judgment* In the passage which comes before us this morning the Apostle turns rather to himself And yet to himself in no sentimental and in no selfish spirit; but entirely as Christ's minister, as one whose personal life is swallowed up and lost in Christ alone. We resume the brief comment at the 12th verse.

But I would ye should understand, brethren[1]. Perhaps there had been contrary rumours. Perhaps the Philippians had thought, as it was natural to think, that the imprisonment of the Apostle must be a great hindrance to the cause of Christ. He is anxious to

[1] *Verse* 12.

correct that impression. He is anxious to shew them that Christ has indeed *all power in heaven and in earth*[1], and can turn even the most opposite influences to His own glory.

That the things which concern me, the events which have befallen me, dangers, persecutions, and now at last a long detention as a prisoner in the great city of Rome, *have come rather to the furtherance of the Gospel* than to its hindrance, have resulted rather in the advancement than in the injury of the cause of Christ God has turned into good that which His enemies designed for evil[2]

So that my bonds became manifest in Christ, under the guiding and controlling hand of Christ, *in all the palace*[3]. The word more properly denotes the camp of the Prætorian guards at Rome; a body of nine or ten thousand men, who were stationed there in a strongly fortified camp for the protection of the capital and of the person of the Emperor. *In all the Prætorian camp, and in all other places;* or rather, *and to all others;* that is, not only among the soldiers of that camp, but among the population of Rome generally. You will remember the description given in the Acts of the Apostles of the arrival of St Paul at Rome. *When we came to Rome, the centurion,* to whose custody he had been committed at Cæsarea, *delivered the prisoners to the captain of the guard*[4], that is, to the

[1] Matt. xxviii. 18.   [2] Gen l 20.   [3] *Verse* 13.   [4] Acts xxviii 16

commander of the Prætorian guards; *but Paul was permitted to dwell by himself with the soldier that kept him*[1]. The hand of the prisoner was fastened by a chain to the hand of the soldier that kept him. This is that *chain* to which St Paul alludes in discourses and letters. *For the hope of Israel I am bound with this chain*[2]... *The mystery of the Gospel, for which I am an ambassador in bonds* · literally, *in a chain*[3]...*He oft refreshed me, and was not ashamed of my chain*[4] We can well understand therefore how St Paul's imprisonment and its cause should become known throughout the Prætorian camp Every change of guard would send back into the camp a soldier whose strange lot it had been to remain for a time actually bound by the hand to this extraordinary prisoner, a witness of necessity to every word which he spoke for Christ, and to every prayer which he breathed to God Was it possible that a strong and wide impression should not thus be produced?

And that many of the brethren in the Lord[5]. The word in the original language is still stronger · *most of the brethren, the brethren in the Lord generally.* *Brethren:* that is what Christians are to each other: brothers and sisters. *In the Lord:* as being all members, component parts, of the same Lord *Waxing confident by my bonds:* literally, *trusting to my bonds:*

[1] Acts xxviii 16.   [2] Acts xxviii. 20.   [3] Eph. vi. 20.
[4] 2 Tim. i. 16   [5] *Verse* 14

emboldened by the sight of my constancy, my safety and my success. *Are much more bold to speak the word without fear* So far from being daunted or discouraged by seeing me a prisoner, it gives them new spirit and new boldness.

Some indeed even from a motive of envy and strife, and some also from a motive of good will, proclaim Christ[1]*: the one*, the latter, *from love, knowing that I am set*, appointed, *for the defence of the Gospel*, and hoping to aid me in it. *but the others*, the former, *from a factious spirit announce Christ, not purely*, not with a sincere motive, *thinking to stir up affliction for my bonds*[2], thinking to add to the distress of my imprisonment. And yet I say, all is well. *For what* is it? what results? *Notwithstanding*, whatever be the motive, *every way, whether in pretence or in truth,* whether in the way of pretext only or from a genuine conviction, *Christ is announced; and in this I rejoice, yea, and will rejoice*[3]. *For I know that this will result to me in salvation*[4]—this trial is one of those *all things* which *work together for good to them that love God*[5]—*through*, by the help of, *your supplication*—you see the value St Paul set upon intercession: he speaks of the prayers of others as one of the instruments of his own salvation[6]—*and the supply of the Spirit of Jesus Christ; according to my earnest expectation and hope,*

---

[1] *Verses* 15, 16.   [2] *Verse* 17   [3] *Verse* 18   [4] *Verse* 19
[5] Rom viii 28   [6] Rom xv 30, 31; 2 Cor i. 10, 11, Philem 22.

that in nothing I shall be ashamed, put to shame by the disappointment of my confidence, *but that in all boldness*, freedom of speech, outspoken frankness in declaring the Gospel, *as always, so now also, Christ shall be magnified in my body, whether by means of life or by means of death*[1].

The general sense of the passage thus minutely rendered may be given thus.

You have heard of my imprisonment. It has lasted now for many months: and the issue of it is altogether doubtful. A sentence of death may at any time close it. In the meantime you may naturally suppose that the effect upon the cause to which my life is devoted has been most disastrous. You imagine me silenced, and you imagine the disciples here daunted and scattered It is quite otherwise[2]. *Christ has overruled these adverse circumstances for an almost unmixed good. The whole camp of the Prætorian guard is familiar with my story. All Rome has heard of the prisoner who is suffering captivity solely for conscience sake*[3]; *solely in the cause of One who was crucified years ago in Judæa, and whom he affirms to be alive*[4] *and to be the appointed Judge of quick and dead. Nay, my imprisonment has emboldened instead of daunting the Christian congregation itself. Taking courage from my example, they are bearing a more manful testimony than before to their*

[1] *Verse* 20
[2] *Verse* 12
[3] *Verse* 13
[4] Acts xxv. 19.

Lord and Master[1]. I wish I could say that this was the simple motive of all who take His name upon their lips. There are some who profess faith and zeal, some who speak the true Gospel with much show of earnestness, who yet know nothing of its elevating and purifying power. They are taking the word out of my lips, in the hope of vexing and provoking me They think that I shall be irritated by finding myself superseded, and that I shall feel my compulsory inactivity the more from seeing my work done by others. Others from a loving motive are helping the great work. They know that the defence of the Gospel is my appointed duty, and that my present suffering is a part of it. They would lighten the load that lies upon me by supplementing my lack of service While I lie still and suffer, they will speak and testify[2]. Thus, from whatever motive, good or evil, Christ's preachers and heralds are multiplied. And, though I would that the hearts of all his professed messengers were pure and honest as the message, I can rejoice in the thought that at all events the message is being carried, the truth witnessed, and my Master honoured[3]. I know that even compulsory inactivity, however trying,—far more trying, when the heart is in earnest, than any toil or any difficulty—and I know that even unkindness, jealousy, and secret enmity, from those who ought to be my friends as they profess to be my fellow-workers—I know that even these things shall

[1] *Verse* 14.   [2] *Verses* 15—17.   [3] *Verse* 18.

work together to the great end, my salvation in the day of Jesus Christ Help me every one of you by your prayers—help me Thou, most of all, my Lord and Saviour, by the constant supply of thy Holy Spirit[1]! So shall my hope be bright, so shall my expectation be stedfast, that everything shall turn to blessing; that I shall never have to say, God hath forgotten or forsaken me; but that whether by joy or by sorrow, whether by diligence or by patience, whether by boldness or by suffering, whether by life or by death, Christ my Lord and Master shall be magnified in my body[2]

Christ magnified in my body.

We all see in some points what St Paul must have meant by this expression It was a thought frequently present with him We find it for example in one of his Epistles to the Church of Corinth, where he speaks of *always bearing about in the body the dying of the Lord Jesus, that the life also of Jesus might be made manifest in his body*[3], in other words, of being made in this world like Jesus in His death, of living as it were a dying life, of *dying daily*[4], as he elsewhere expresses it—of holding his life always in his hands, having it constantly threatened and battered and undermined, and expecting it day by day to be actually taken away—that so the life of Jesus, His risen life, the power of His resurrection and of His constant

---

[1] *Verse* 19.   [2] *Verse* 20
[3] 2 Cor. iv. 10.   [4] 1 Cor. xv. 31.

presence in His people, may be displayed in him, shewn forth, in its marvellous strength and reality, by enabling him to suffer on and yet also to live on; to bear anything and everything, and to be destroyed by nothing, until the appointed day of his change come, and he who has been faithful on earth unto death is admitted into the life which is above death and beyond death for ever. This is something of what is expressed when he says that Christ shall be magnified in his body, whether by life or by death. If he lives, if his earthly life is protracted through toils so constant and sufferings so intense, this shews the supporting hand of the risen, the immortal Saviour. There must be some marvellous power out of and above him, or he must long ago have sunk under such pressure. There must be One above, who comforts him under all his tribulation[1]. There must be One above, who communicates a strength not his own to do and to suffer for His sake. There must be One above, whose grace is sufficient for him[2], sufficient to keep him meek under provocation, courageous under intimidation, and stedfast in the face of danger. Christ is thus magnified (not made great, but shewn to be great) in his body by life. And if death comes, as come it must one day, to close his course; if confession is to end in martyrdom, and many hairbreadth escapes are to issue in a death by violence; then He who gives courage

[1] 2 Cor. 1 4.   [2] 2 Cor. xii. 9.

still, gives comfort still, gives hope and patience, love and gratitude still, will then not least but most be honoured and magnified in his body; he who gives his life gives his all, and the poor tortured mangled frame shall be itself not more a sacrifice to Christ's glory than a testimony to Christ's power Christ who makes him willing to die for Him, Christ who gives him grace, courage and constancy to die for Him, shall be magnified in him still, magnified in his body, as by life, so by death.

Such was the meaning of the words before us for St Paul himself. Have they any meaning for us also, my beloved brethren? for us who live in days when the fires of martyrdom are extinguished, and when the still more tremendous conflicts of the latter day have not yet set in? Let us bring them home to our own circumstances, to our own lives, to our own hearts, and what do they say?

Christ shall be magnified in my body. It is in the power of a Christian—so the words import—to magnify Christ, that is, to shew the greatness of Christ, in his body. We can all think of some ways of doing this

Shall I speak of temperance? of the manner in which a true Christian eats and drinks to God's glory[1]? of the moderation, yet also of the deep thankfulness, with which he partakes of God's good gifts to the body,

---

[1] 1 Cor. x. 31.

his food, his clothing, his sleep, his home? how he enjoys all even above other men, just because he sees something in all, some One through and above all, unseen and unregarded by others around him, who are altogether forgetting the Giver in the gift? how too he acts upon his Saviour's maxim, *But rather*—instead of torturing yourselves with petty questions of ceremonial scrupulosity as to the use of God's creatures—*give alms of such things as ye have, and, behold, all things are clean unto you*[1], in other words, the way to partake of God's gifts without defilement is to share them with those who lack · let your abundance minister to another's want[2], be always ready to listen to the call of charity, and if it call not, listen for it and forestall it, and then, *behold, all things are clean unto you*. This is one way, now and in all times, of magnifying Christ in your body.

Or shall I speak of purity? of the struggle which a Christian, in the name and strength of Christ, has evermore to maintain with the lusts of the flesh? how he sets himself by prayer and watchfulness to coerce the first risings of evil desire, and to live in pureness as well as in temperance?

Or shall I speak of his activity? how a Christian sets himself, in the name of Christ, and in a spirit of deep gratitude for His redemption, to lead a useful and a vigorous life; not yielding to the temptation of

---

[1] Luke xi. 41. [2] 2 Cor. viii 14.

indolence, when it says, *Take thine ease, eat, drink, and be merry*[1], but endeavouring day by day to do some strong active work in the service of his generation and to the honour and glory of God? This too, if it be done in a right spirit, is a magnifying of Christ in the body: and over that man's grave, when at last he rests in Jesus, shall be inscribed, as by the finger of Christ, that humblest yet noblest epitaph, *He served his own generation by the will of God, and then fell on sleep*[2].

But there are yet two ways in which a Christian is sure to be called to magnify Christ in his body, besides those more common ones which have thus far been mentioned.

One of these is suffering Every one of us has or will have something to bear; something which makes a demand upon his fortitude, upon his patience, upon his submission, upon his temper, upon his Christian charity It may be ill health, it may be disappointment; it may be failure in his business or in his profession; it may be loss of friends; it may be compulsory solitude; it may be depression of spirits; it may be great anxiety; it may be forced inaction. It must at last, in all probability, be pain; bodily distress, ending in agony, in anguish Now in all these things Christ may be magnified, or Christ may be dishonoured. He is dishonoured by fretfulness, by

[1] Luke xii. 19.   [2] Acts xiii 36

repining, by dwelling upon past happiness, by a dejection which refuses to be comforted. He is magnified by a manly and a Christian composure; by a resignation gradually brightened into cheerfulness; by a courageous hope, and by a stedfast expectation.

And then at last death has to be borne. And I need not say to any one here present, how little we the living know of that thing itself of which the name is so familiar. It is a secret thing; a thing which no man knows save by once for all passing through it himself. When it comes, as come it must, to each one of us, may we be enabled like St Paul to magnify Christ in it. Nothing magnifies Christ like a Christian deathbed; when all murmuring and all complaining being far removed, there is a perfect submission of the will, and an entire repose of the heart, and an unquestioning affiance of the soul, all based upon what Christ has done, and upon what Christ has promised, and above all upon what Christ is. When a man can really find peace then from a tortured body and from an agitated mind, in the long-tried support and comfort of a Saviour who died for him and rose again, he pays a tribute to His greatness and to His truth and to His character, at once the noblest and the last. *Christ shall be magnified in my body, whether it be by life or by death.*

That it may be so in these later senses, let us set ourselves to magnify Christ in the earlier. By temperance, by pureness, and by Christian diligence, let us endeavour to shew forth what He is, that others also may take knowledge of Him and feel His glory. And this day reminds us that there is one way, simple but real, in which, while life and health last, we ought to be magnifying Christ by our body. There is one act of worship, in which the body takes part At the Lord's Table we shew forth in outward sign what our hearts think of Christ, and what Christ is to us. O let us not refuse that homage! Let us not be remiss, irregular, or intermittent, in announcing the Lord's death, not by word, but by act, until His coming again[1]! Then, above other times, we echo those solemn, those touching words of the same Apostle who speaks to us in the text, *None of us liveth to himself, and no man dieth to himself. For whether we live, we live unto the Lord; and whether we die, we die unto the Lord: whether we live therefore or die, we are the Lord's For to this end Christ both died, and rose, and revived, that He might be Lord both of the dead and living*[2].

[1] 1 Cor. xi. 26.   [2] Rom. xiv 7—9

TWENTY-THIRD SUNDAY AFTER TRINITY,
November 3, 1861.

LECTURE IV.

PHILIPPIANS I 21—26

21   *For to me to live is Christ, and to have died is gain.*
22 *And if to live in flesh [is appointed for me], this is to me*
   a fruit of labour: and what I shall choose I declare not
23 *And I am perplexed by the two; having my desire unto the*
   having departed and being with Christ · for it is much
24 *rather preferable: but to stay on in the flesh is more neces-*
25 *sary for your sake.   And believing this I know that I shall*
   remain, and remain along with you all, unto your progress
26 *and joy of the faith; that your triumph may abound in*
   Christ Jesus in me by means of my presence again with you

LECTURE IV.

PHILIPPIANS I 21.

To me to live is Christ and to die is gain

As always, so now also, Christ shall be magnified in my body, whether it be by life or by death. Those were the last words dwelt upon. To-day we have the reason for this confidence. Everything shall turn out well with him, compulsory inaction, irksome imprisonment, impending danger, yes, if so it be, even death itself; in all these things it shall be well for him, and well for the cause of Christ also; because to him *to live is Christ, and to die*, or more exactly, *to have died, is gain*[1] *To have died.* It is not the act of dying which is gain to any man. Many unreal things have been written by the ignorant living as to *the bliss of dying.* It is not dying which is bliss, but the having died; the having gone through that which is in itself all-humiliating and all-painful, into the clear light and into the perfect peace beyond.

[1] *Verse* 21.

St Paul is pondering an alternative. He has said, *whether by life or by death* He now says what life is to him, and what death will be to him. And he proceeds to balance the two possibilities. He may die, or he may live. The result of his imprisonment was still in doubt. He puts first the alternative of life; of an escape from his present imprisonment, not through death, but into prolonged life *And if to live in flesh —to live on,* to continue in life—if to live on in this bodily life is appointed for me, *this is to me a fruit of labour*[1]; this will have the advantage of enabling me to labour: if I live on, I can also work on. St Paul loved work for its own sake Most people work for the sake of the results of work; work that they may gain by working; gain a livelihood, or gain a position, or gain a fortune, or gain rank and fame St Paul called work itself a *fruit* or advantage. He worked for the work's sake What had he to gain by it? In this world nothing: in a worldly sense, less than nothing: things which were gain to him—advantages of which his countrymen, of which he himself in earlier days, thought highly—these things he had cast away for Christ[2]. But he had learned that none of these things was worth keeping: he had learned to count work for Christ its own reward: and if he looked forward to continued life, it was only because it would give him what he calls *the fruit of work;* the advan-

[1] *Verse 22.*   [2] Phil iii. 7.

tage of working on yet a little longer before the night should come when work would be impossible[1].

And what I shall choose—which of the two possibilities I should select if the choice between life and death were allowed me—*I declare not* · that is, as we say, I cannot tell. There is so much to be said on both sides, so much in favour of living on, and so much in favour of death; that I cannot say which of the two I should decide for, if I might take which I would

And I am perplexed by the two: more exactly, *I am painfully cramped and straitened by the pressure of the two things*[2], life and death, plying me with their conflicting claims, the one saying, Think of this, and the other saying, Think of that, each urging its case, and clamouring for a decision.

Having my desire—my desire being—*unto the having departed and being with Christ;* that being the aim and object of my desire. The word here used for *departing* is taken from the loosing of the cables which bind a vessel to the shore till the moment of its sailing: then the rope is untied or broken, and the ship weighs anchor St Paul's desire, the preference of his will, was in favour of starting at once on that brief voyage across the narrow sea of death, which would bring him to *the haven where he would be*[3], even to the everlasting presence of his loved Lord and Saviour.

[1] John ix 4.   [2] *Verse* 23.   [3] Ps cvii. 30

Having my desire unto departing and being with Christ: for it is far more preferable. There is a double comparative: literally, *by much more better.*

That is his personal choice. *But to remain on in the flesh is more necessary for your sake*[1]. To go is pleasanter: to stay is more necessary; more urgently required for your sake. It is not so necessary that I should be at once in heaven, as it is that I should still serve you on earth. I had rather go. but, when I think of you, I had better stay. A Christian has not only to think of what would be best for himself: he must consider also how he can do most good to others My brethren, a man who really desires to be with Christ, and yet for the sake of others prefers to stay on earth, sets us an example of unselfishness which may well arouse in us some serious thoughts It is very easy for a man who does not care to be with Christ to say, I hope for my children's sake God will spare me a little longer before I go hence and be no more seen: that is nothing. But when a man is eager, like St Paul, for his great change, then to think of others; then to choose earth rather than heaven because of good that may thus be done; is a rare exercise of unselfishness. There have been those who have come back with regret from the gates of death; who have sighed at the physician's announcement that their time is not yet come; and they may enter, as few of

[1] *Verse* 24.

us are able to do, into the greatness of the sacrifice which breathes in these words

And believing this, in this confidence, being assured that your good requires my continuance on earth, *I know that I shall remain, and remain along with you all, unto your progress and joy of the faith*[1]*;* so as to advance you, by my sympathy, counsel, and prayers, on your heavenward way, and so as also to *help your joy*[2] in believing, to make you happier as well as holier, *that your triumph*[3]—properly, the subject of your triumphing, that in which you triumph or glory, namely your participation in the Gospel and all that is involved in it—*may abound,* may be made yet more real and satisfying to you, *in Christ Jesus,* by the help and blessing of that Saviour in whom you are incorporated, *in me,* that is, under my ministry, *by means of my presence again with you.* I hope that your comfort and joy in the Gospel may be largely increased by the instrumentality of that future presence amongst you, to which I now confidently look forward[4].

Let me briefly paraphrase for you the verses on which we have dwelt.

I spoke of a conviction that whatever happens to me will turn to Christ's glory Life or death can make no difference there. What is my life? It is, in one word, Christ; not this or that about Christ; not His service

---

[1] *Verse* 25. [2] 2 Cor 1. 24.
[3] *Verse* 26. [4] Rom. 1. 11, 12

only, or His will only, or His power only; it is Christ Himself. And what is my death? Will that be no glory to Christ? Will that lie beyond the sphere of His notice or of His concern? Nay, death, even more than life, will cement my tie to Him: life to me is Christ, but even beyond that, death to me shall be a gain. It shall give me what life itself could not give even to one whose very life is Christ[1]. What then is before me? Life? prolonged life on earth? It is well. Life lengthened is lengthened work; work sweet in itself, and glorious in its recompenses. What shall I say? Which of the two, life or death, shall I choose if choice be mine[2]? How difficult, how perplexing a decision! I know indeed which way my wish inclines: better were it, far better, for me myself, to depart hence and to be with Christ Gladly would I loose the cables of flesh and sense, and however stormy the sea which must be traversed, commit myself to His guidance who awaits me on the shore beyond[3]. There to be for ever with the Lord[4] must be a blessedness to which the life even of faith aspires not But there are other things more urgent than my selfish happiness: there are souls to be counselled and comforted, there are congregations to be watched over and visited. You yourselves want me: my work for you is not yet completed. It will be time enough for rest when labour is ended: for the present

[1] *Verse* 21.   [2] *Verse* 22.
[3] *Verse* 23   [4] 1 Thess. iv. 17.

IV.]　　　　　　*CHAP. I.* 21—26.　　　　　　61

I have work to do; a work which I cannot depute, a work not ripe for transmission[1]. *Surely He in whose hand I am will order for me a longer continuance. Surely I shall be preserved to help you under burdens which oppress and amidst difficulties which surround you*[2]. *Yes, I shall see you again; and your joy in the Gospel shall be made yet more abundant by renewed intercourse with him who first spoke to you of a Saviour, and who can tell from his own experience alike of the infirmities of nature and of the upholding strength of Christ*[3].

To me to live is Christ The connection in which these words stand seems to give as their primary meaning, The business of my life is Christ. my energy, my activity, my occupation, my interest, is all Christ. Let us take this thought first Just as our Lord Himself, when He was at length found in the temple, said to His parents, *Wist ye not that I must be about my Father's business*[4]? *knew ye not that I must be in*, be engrossed and absorbed in, *the things of my Father?* even so St Paul says here that the business of his life is Christ : he is in, exists in, lives only for, the things of Christ. He regarded everything that he had to do, and he regarded everything that befell him, only in relation to, in its bearing upon, Christ. His question was, not, How can I get on in life? how can I get one

[1] *Verse* 24.　　　[2] *Verse* 25
[3] *Verse* 26.　　　[4] Luke 11 49

step higher? how can I add to my income? how can I outstrip this rival, or supplant that competitor? none of these things influenced him: he had given up all this world's advancements, he had renounced all this world's ambitions: his question in everything was, What will serve the cause of Christ? what course of conduct, what journey or what letter, will help to make Christ more known, more regarded, more loved on earth? In this sense, first of all, to him to live was Christ.

My brethren, it is almost alarming to write or to utter such words as these. They describe a condition so widely different from that of most of us. As a mere expression of theological doctrine, as a mere narrative of how certain men lived and felt eighteen hundred years ago, it does not startle, it does not shock us: but O let us ask ourselves, In what did those men differ from us? Was it more necessary then to be holy, to be devoted, to be Christian men, than it is now? Was heaven in those days harder to win, or did God ask of His creatures then a kind or a degree of obedience which He has now ceased to look for? Force yourselves to entertain these questions: they are salutary, they are needful, for us all. And if the answer be, as it must be in its first sound, severe and condemning, yet let us not put it from us. Rather let us give entrance to it as to a new conviction, and consider calmly with ourselves what we can do in consequence of it. To a Christian, it says, the business of life is Christ: first therefore, he must take care that Christ is not utterly excluded from his practical life: he must begin by thinking of Him, by going in quest of Him, by praying to Him, by asking Him to be his life, by giving up anything which he knows Christ could not approve and could not dwell with, by making (if I might so express it) a clear space, a clean place, for Christ in his heart, and by being jealous over himself lest in reality his whole work and his whole pleasure in life be utterly severed from Christ and exclusive of Him. It is a first step—and let me say, it is more than half way towards being a Christian altogether—when a man sets himself to think of Christ, to invite Him into his life, and to consider how to avoid in some definite respects displeasing and dishonouring Him. Christ cannot possibly be everything to us, without first being something to us: and to many—to some, it may be, even in this congregation—what is He in reality but a notion or a name?

Before St Paul could say that his outward life was Christ, he must have been able to say it of his inward life Before Christ can be to any one his object, his business, his work, in life, He must first be his trust and his hope, his known and tried refuge from guilt, from fear, from restlessness, from sin. When St Paul writes here, *To me to live is Christ*, we cannot but remember those other words of his to the Galatians, *And it is no longer I that live, but Christ liveth in me*[1]*;* or again, to the Colossians, *Ye are dead,* or rather, *ye died;* that is, when Christ died, ye died with Him; *and your life is hid with Christ in God: when Christ who is our life shall appear, then shall ye also appear with him in glory*[2] Yes, the inward, in this sense, comes before the outward A man must have Christ for the life of his soul, before he can have Christ for the life of his life He must enter into the meaning of our Lord's own words, *I am the bread of life: he that cometh to me shall never hunger, and he that believeth on me shall never thirst*[3] And is it not here that we are most defective ? Small as is the regard paid in our life to Christ, is there not even less of regard for Him in our souls? Yes, I would repeat and press home the enquiry, though God alone and your own hearts can read the answer to it, Which of us knows what it is to have Christ, by His Holy Spirit, for the stay and the comfort, the strength and the happiness, of his own soul within ? Which of us is even seeking to know Him thus by faith ? Which of us has any real vital religion, beyond a few forms of worship, and a few rules of a conventional morality ? Which of us lives differently, as to his secret thoughts and feelings, from what he would have done if Christ had never lived, never died, or never risen ? I ask these things, not (God knows)

[1] Gal. ii 20. [2] Col. iii. 3, 4 [3] John vi 35

in a spirit of harshness or of fancied superiority, but in a spirit of sincere concern and of tender sympathy. For indeed, if our Saviour's blood was shed for us, and if He really spoke on earth the words which His Evangelists, and more especially which St John, have recorded, there must be something wrong, something dangerous, in living as to our soul's deepest thoughts without or apart from Him: we must be incurring the just condemnation conveyed in those alarming words of the Baptist, *He that believeth on the Son hath everlasting life; and he that believeth not the Son shall not see life, but the wrath of God abideth on him*[1].

To St Paul—and in this respect St Paul was but an example for the humblest Christian—to St Paul, inwardly first, and then outwardly—in soul first, and then in action—*to live was Christ* And therefore, therefore only, was he able to add in truth and soberness, *And to me to die is gain.* Painful in itself, as to all of us, painful in his case even beyond ours—for he, when he thus wrote, expected life to be closed, as it was closed a few years later, by a death of martyrdom, yet that death, consummated and endured, was a gain to him even in comparison with a Christian's life. Here to live was Christ: but even beyond that there was a blessedness into which only death could usher him. *To have died is gain.* To have died is to have done with weariness, with

[1] John iii. 36.

distraction, with anxiety, with fear, with sickness, with pain, with grief, with separation, for ever. To have died is to have done with infirmity, to have done with temptation, to have done with sin. *He that has died is freed from sin*[1]. All these things may have passed across St Paul's mind when he wrote down the words of the text. But no one of them has he recorded. One thing, one only, has he thought worth uttering; one thing, before the glory of which all other lustre must have paled and been extinguished, *I have a desire to depart and to be with Christ* It is of this last thing that he writes, *which is far better Therefore we are always confident*, he writes elsewhere to the Corinthians, *knowing that, whilst we are at home in the body, we are absent from the Lord, for we walk by faith, not by sight; we are confident, I say, and willing rather to be absent from the body, and to be present with the Lord. wherefore we labour that, whether present or absent, we may be accepted of Him*[2]

My brethren, if we would die the Christian's death, we must live the Christian's life. If we would find it a gain to have died, we must have found it to us Christ to live God grant that the thoughts here suggested may quicken some of us to deep thought, to serious questioning, to a conversion of heart, to a transformation of life! It may come to us, even each one of

[1] Rom vi 7.   [2] 2 Cor. v. 6—9.

these things, more quickly than we either ask or think. But if it tarry, wait for it: it will surely come at last, and will not for ever tarry[1]. Then shall you rejoice that you acquiesced not in any substitute for faith, in any counterfeit of the life of Christ: you will say then that it was worth waiting for, worth praying for, worth suffering for. If never on this earth you shall rise to the full glory of the Christian standing, at least, if you struggle on till death and faint not, you shall depart to be with Christ, and be satisfied, when you awake, with His likeness[2].

[1] Hab ii 3. [2] Psalm xvii. 15.

TWENTY-FIFTH SUNDAY AFTER TRINITY,
November 17, 1861.

LECTURE V.

PHILIPPIANS I. 27—30.

27   ONLY *live (as citizens) worthily of the Gospel of Christ,
that whether coming and seeing you* [*I may observe,*] *or being
absent I may hear of the things which concern you, that ye
stand fast in one spirit, with one soul striving together with*
28 *the faith of the Gospel, and not scared in anything by your
adversaries, which is to them a proof of perdition, but to you*
29 *of salvation, and that from God.   For to you it was granted,
in behalf of Christ—not only to believe on Him, but also—to*
30 *suffer in behalf of Him; ye having the same struggle such as
ye saw in me and now hear of in me.*

LECTURE V.

PHILIPPIANS I. 27.

Only let your conversation be as it becometh the Gospel of Christ

I HAD *rather go: but I had better stay. To depart at once and be with Christ is in itself preferable. To one whose life has been Christ, death must be gain But when I think of you, I feel that it would be selfish to choose an immediate release. And if my work is not ended, I am persuaded that He who is the Lord of life and death will appoint for me a longer continuance. I shall see you again—such is my confidence—to further your faith and to help your joy.*

Only[1], thus the text opens, *only*, whether my present peril ends thus or thus, ends in life or ends in death, ends in my preservation to see you again or ends in my withdrawal from the labours and responsibilities of this world, whichever of the two be

[1] *Verse* 27.

the result which God shall ordain, *let your conversation be as it becometh the Gospel of Christ.* The word *conversation* has now a more restricted meaning. In Scripture it denotes conduct: with us it denotes language. The words of the text would be more exactly, *Only live worthily of the Gospel of Christ.* And there is a further force in the expression. *Live*, is properly, *live as citizens; use your citizenship:* you Christians are citizens; you have a city, a glorious and heavenly city, of which the franchise is yours; you have rights and privileges in that connection; then use your citizenship in a particular way, a way briefly here described as being *worthy of the Gospel of Christ.*

The same word is found in a well-known passage in the Acts of the Apostles. *Paul, earnestly beholding the council, said, Men and brethren, I have lived in all good conscience before God until this day*[1]. The exact expression there also is, *I have lived as a citizen unto God*, I have used my citizenship in the sight of God, *in all good conscience*, in the maintenance of a strictly conscientious principle in all respects. And once again, in a later chapter of this Epistle, we have a kindred word to that employed in the text: *For our conversation*, literally *our citizenship, is in heaven*[2].

We are not refining therefore beyond St Paul's real meaning, when we say that the text imports this:

[1] Acts xxiii. 1. [2] Phil. iii. 20.

Use your citizenship, live as citizens of the heavenly city, in a manner worthy of the Gospel of Christ. Thus the same Apostle writes to the Ephesians, *I beseech you that ye walk worthy of the vocation (calling) wherewith ye were called*[1]*;* and to the Colossians, *That ye might walk worthy of the Lord unto all pleasing*[2]*;* and to the Thessalonians, *That ye would walk worthy of God, who calleth you unto (into) His own kingdom and glory*[3]. In a manner worthy of your calling; worthy of the Lord; worthy of God; and now here, worthy of the Gospel of Christ. This will be the topic of our concluding remarks.

That whether coming and seeing you, or else being absent, I may hear of the things which concern you, that ye stand fast in one spirit, with one soul striving together with the faith of the Gospel. That whether by coming and seeing you I may observe, or in continued absence I may hear, with respect to your spiritual condition, that you are still stedfast in one spirit, without jar or discord, with one united soul struggling along with the faith of the Gospel; that is, joining all your efforts with those of the struggling Gospel; giving your vigorous, your strenuous aid to that faith which the Gospel teaches. *Striving together with,* not *for, the faith of,* revealed and taught by, *the Gospel* The expression may remind us of that contained in the description of charity or Christian love in the first

[1] Eph. iv. 1   [2] Col i 10.   [3] 1 Thess. ii 12.

Epistle to the Corinthians: *rejoiceth not in iniquity, but rejoiceth with the truth*[1]; sympathizes, that is, in the joy of the truth, in the success, the prosperity, the triumph, of the truth or Gospel.

There is one word of application here, which will have suggested itself to all our minds. First of all, Am I really in sympathy with the Gospel? on the side of the Gospel? concerned, interested, involved, in its cause? And then again, Do I at all enter into the thought of its being (as the word here used imports) a struggle, a contest, a sort of wrestling for a prize—that is the figure—to side thus with the Gospel? What do any of us know of exertion in the cause of Christ? of vigorous, anxious, earnest effort in taking the part of Christ in the world? a struggle first with sin, then with self, then, and only in the third place, with opposition from without?

And not terrified in anything by your adversaries[2] The word is particularly applied to horses; *shying* at some unexpected and formidable object. How many of our fears deserve no better name! What imaginary terrors do we start aside from in our Christian course! Walk up to them, face them, survey them steadily, and they vanish, they are not. How often have we thought, I can never brace myself to say this which I ought to say, or to shew my convictions before this person or that, of whom I am so much afraid; and

---

[1] 1 Cor. xiii. 6. [2] *Verse* 28.

yet if with prayer and resolution, in humility and in faith, we have made the effort, we have found it quite easy! *When they looked, they saw that the stone was rolled away: for it was very great*[1]. So will it be with all the dangers and with all the adversaries that Christ calls us to encounter. *Be scared in nothing by your adversaries.*

Which opposition *is to them a proof of perdition, but to you of salvation, and that from God.* The thought is remarkable. St Paul here tells us what opposition on the part of any person to Christ and His true servants really indicates. Two things perdition to the opposer, and salvation to the opposed. To fight against Christ, quite apart from the question of its present apparent success or failure, is a sign of ruin to him who is guilty of it You may be quite sure that you are a doomed man if you, a creature, are fighting against your own Creator. *Woe unto him that striveth with his Maker*[2]*!* If there is anything which Christ has said and which you are resisting, you may be quite sure that you are resisting it to your own ruin. *It is hard for thee to kick against the goad*[3]. And if there be any person who is humbly and earnestly serving or trying to serve Christ, and you thwart, ridicule or tempt that person, whether you succeed or fail in your object, you may be quite sure that you have upon you the mark of perdition: you must perish if you fight

---

[1] Mark xvi. 4. [2] Isai. xlv. 9. [3] Acts xxvi. 14.

against Christ. On the other hand, to be opposed, to be disliked, to be threatened or molested, in trying to serve Christ, has this special blessing upon it: it is a proof of salvation: it is a mark of belonging to Christ, and they who belong to Him are for ever safe, for ever happy. This is the heavenly view of earthly persecution. He who sees the end from the beginning regards opposition to Christ's servants, whatever its immediate result, as a mark in itself of perdition on the part of the agent, and of salvation on the part of the sufferer[1]. And St Paul was enlightened to see it in the same divine light.

For to you it was granted, in behalf of Christ— not only to believe on Him, but also—to suffer in behalf of Him[2]. *Given*, he says: given (the word imports) as a favour, as a special boon. Such is the Christian view of suffering. It is an added favour, over and above the gift of faith. The sentence begins as if it should proceed at once, *it was given, in behalf of Christ to suffer:* the words *not only to believe on Him, but also*, are an interruption, after which *in behalf of Him* is repeated to repair the breach.

Having the same struggle such as ye saw in me[3] when I was with you; the same conflict, the same contest, the same *fight of afflictions*[4] and of persecutions, which ye then *saw in me*, in my case, *and*

---

[1] Compare 2 Thess. 1 4—10.
[2] *Verse* 29.
[3] *Verse* 30.
[4] Heb x. 32.

now hear of in me. The word here rendered *conflict* is that which occurs elsewhere with very various translations *We were bold in our God to speak unto you the Gospel of God with much* contention[1]...*Fight the good* fight *of faith*[2]...*I have fought the good* fight[3] ...*Let us run with patience the* race *that is set before us*[4]. It is a word of which the leading idea is strenuous effort, whether it be shewn in contending for a prize, in enduring persecution or anguish, or as sometimes, in maintaining amidst all discouragements the work of persevering prayer.

We have reached the close of the first Chapter. And I will now, as before, endeavour to give in a brief paraphrase the sense of the four verses on which we have dwelt to-day.

I may come to you, or I may not come[5]: *I cannot tell; God knoweth. But however this be, your duty, your privilege, your Christian life, are yours, not mine, to guard and to exercise. Citizens of a better country, that is an heavenly*[6], *live your citizenship! Remember your King, remember your fellow-citizens, remember your capital and your home. Live as those should live who have a Gospel; a message of joyful intelligence, a summons of lofty promise, a calling full of immortality. Disgrace not your Gospel. Forfeit it not for yourselves: disparage it not in the eyes of others. Let*

---

[1] 1 Thess. ii 2. [2] 1 Tim. vi. 12. [3] 2 Tim. iv. 7.
[4] Heb. xii. 1. [5] *Verse* 27. [6] Heb. xi. 16.

your life, inward and outward, be worthy of the Gospel of Christ So, if I come, I shall find you such as I would: if I come not, I shall hear of you that which I desire. I shall hear that you are not gone backward from a standing once attained I shall hear that you are stedfast at the post assigned you; and that, not as single isolated combatants, but as a united body animated by a common spirit. I shall hear that you regard the cause of Christ as your cause, and that you give to it the support not of a cold-hearted acquiescence, but of an earnest and devoted exertion. And what if in this struggle you find, as you will find, adversaries? They will not scare you by their menaces, they will not intimidate you by their violence[1] *you will meet them with a calm resolution, and view them with an eye on which the light of eternity has risen You will see in them not your foes, but the foes of Christ; and you will find in every instance of their hostility an added proof of your safety and of their danger. No weapon forged against Christ can prosper*[2]*: if the thing formed rises against Him that formed it, it must be with an onset at once impotent and suicidal. Happy they to whom, as to you, it is granted to be Christ's champions*[3]*! To them suffering itself is not a sign of desertion but of acceptance and of honour. Even more than faith itself, it marks them out as heirs of salvation. You saw, when I was with you, you hear now in my absence,*

[1] *Verse* 28 [2] Isai. liv. 17. [3] *Verse* 29.

what my lot is in these matters: in this, as in all else, you and I are one[1].

And now I will ask you to turn back, in conclusion, to the few words read as the text, and to ask with all seriousness, what do these words say to us who are here assembled to-day?

Only let your conversation be as it becometh the Gospel of Christ. Only live your citizenship in a manner worthy of the Gospel of Christ. It is plain that every precept of holy living might be brought under this comprehensive charge. And for this sort of detail we have no space Let us narrow the compass of the exhortation Let us say, Live inwardly, and live outwardly, as citizens of that kingdom which the Gospel has revealed

1. How large a part of life is lived wholly within Public life, social life, family life, these do not exhaust the whole being even in those who are most busy, most sociable, or most domestic Within and beside all these there is for all of us a life yet more real, yet more important And the danger of all those other kinds of life is lest they should obscure or paralyze or stifle this It is for our soul's sake, for our eternal welfare's sake, that we must watch and pray against this danger. As *the heart knoweth his own bitterness, and a stranger doth not intermeddle with his joy*[2]; as in some senses therefore we all have a secret life which we

[1] *Verse* 30.   [2] Prov. xiv. 10.

cannot part with nor make public even if we would, so it is our great business to attend to this secret life, to regulate and cultivate it, in such a way as that it may become, as it is here expressed, worthy of the Gospel.

And how shall this be? We might express it in many ways. But any one mode of expression, if it be true, that is if it be consistent with Scripture, will suffice for the purpose. Let us say then that we ought to be living our citizenship inwardly towards Christ our Lord and King. The state of our mind towards Him personally ought to be that which suits and is consistent with our relation to Him as His subjects. There are those who laugh at states of mind, at inward feelings and dispositions, altogether. And no doubt these things may be too much talked of they may be fantastic, or they may be morbid: they may be too minutely scrutinized or too confidently and indolently trusted in. But none the less is it true that all religion must begin with the heart; that all faith, however active, however practical, has and must have its root and its life within. I would suggest then for your consideration to-day, my brethren, this question. Is my mind towards Christ that which becomes His Gospel? Is He anything to me? Have I any real conviction of His being, of His work, of His living power, of His heart-searching judgment? I much fear that there may be some here present who cannot answer that question satisfactorily. We hear from time to time things which shew us decisively how little we can trust to the mere profession of faith made by worshipping in this congregation. When the curtain is lifted for a moment, whether in life or in death, from some heart which has passed amongst us with a tolerable character for morality or even for religion, how terrible sometimes, how appalling, is the disclosure! If there be present this morning but one person in whose ear the word sounds with alarming truthfulness, let him not put it from him Let him whose heart is ever so distant from God, let him whose life is ever so much stained and defiled with sin, yet fall upon his knees, when he returns home from this service, and entreat God for Christ's sake to convince, to convert, to save him. O do not drift further down the stream, do not float nearer to the great Ocean, without one earnest effort to shake off the sin which besets and to take refuge in the Saviour who redeemed you!

2. And then that which is within will shine through into that which is without also. He whose inner life is that of one whom Christ has saved will be living outwardly also as a citizen of the *kingdom not of this world*[1]. His aims and his motives will be higher than those of men who know not God. He will not be a worldly man. He will not be a vain

[1] John xviii 36.

man. He will not be a trifling man. He will not be a man of words only. He will *declare plainly* by his acts also that he is one who *seeks a country*[1]. Let me say, above all, that he will be one who recognizes others as his fellow-citizens and his brethren, one who desires that they also should walk worthily of the Gospel, one who cares for their souls, and keeps himself with all diligence both in word and deed lest he injure, lest he corrupt, lest he defile that soul or that body of another for which, even as for his own, Christ his Lord and his King submitted patiently to the very pangs of death.

God of His infinite mercy carry the feeble word of man with power into the heart that needs it! May He, even as He has promised, make His Word *as the hammer that breaketh the rock in pieces*[2], and turn the hard wayside[3] of the most sinful heart into that deep and soft and fertile soil which gives the seed a ready entrance and blesses it with an abundant harvest!

[1] Heb. xi. 14.   [2] Jer xxiii. 29   [3] Matt xiii. 19

SUNDAY NEXT BEFORE ADVENT,
November 24, 1861.

LECTURE VI.

PHILIPPIANS II. 1—4.

1 *IF there be therefore any consolation in Christ, if any*
2 *comfort of love, if any fellowship of the Spirit, if any tenderness and compassions, fulfil my joy, that ye be of the same*
3 *mind, having the same love, of one soul, of one mind, not at all according to party-spirit, nor according to vainglory, but in your humility accounting each other superior to your-*
4 *selves; not regarding each of you your own things, but each of you also the things of others.*

LECTURE VI.

PHILIPPIANS II. 2.

Fulfil ye my joy, that ye be likeminded.

IN almost every respect St Paul's language to the Philippian congregation is one of thankfulness and satisfaction. He addresses them, not only as called and chosen[1], but also as loving and faithful. He can thank God upon every remembrance of them, and is confident that He who hath begun a good work in them will perform it in the day of Jesus Christ[2].

There was just one point, as to which, from the very earnestness of his exhortations upon it, we may infer that he felt some anxiety. The four verses which I purpose to bring before you this morning enter into the very heart of this subject. I will first read and paraphrase the passage itself, and then seek to draw from it its deep instruction; an instruction as needful for these days and for this congregation as

[1] Rev. xvii. 14.   [2] Phil. i 3, 6.

ever it was for the church of Philippi and for the first century of the Gospel. May He be with us, whose blessing alone can make His own Word fruitful!

If there be therefore any consolation in Christ, if any comfort of love, if any fellowship of the Spirit, if any tenderness and compassions[1], *fulfil my joy, that ye be of the same mind, having the same love, of one soul, of one mind*[2].

He has spoken of their faith in Christ, and of their patience in suffering for Christ[3]. And yet there remains something to which they must be exhorted. The exhortation is prefaced by a very strong appeal. The first verse contains a sort of enumeration of motives. As though he had said, I beseech you, brethren, by every blessing and by every privilege which you enjoy as Christians. *If there be any consolation in Christ*[4], is, in other words, I beseech you by whatever consolation there is in Christ; by all the refreshment and by all the repose which your hearts find in Christ; in believing in Christ, in belonging to Christ, in being enveloped and incorporated in Christ. The argument, you perceive, is only vocal to a Christian. It presupposes that we know for ourselves that there is such a thing as consolation in Christ; that we have found for ourselves in Him that rest of spirit which He promises to all who come to Him[5].

[1] *Verse* 1. [2] *Verse* 2. [3] Phil. i. 29
[4] *Verse* 1. [5] Matt. xi. 28.

And then it uses that experience as a motive for a particular effort, a particular attainment, which is to follow.

Again, *if any comfort of love* If there be such a thing as comfort in loving and in being loved by Christ and His people. That is the meaning of this second clause. I beseech you by any comfort which Christians find in loving Christ and in being loved by Christ; in loving their Christian friends and in being loved by them.

In the third place, *if any fellowship of the Spirit* You remember the benediction at the close of the second Epistle to the Corinthians; that benediction which concludes our service: *The grace of the Lord Jesus Christ, and the love of God, and the communion (fellowship) of the Holy Ghost, be with you all*[1]. The word is the same here. *If there be any communion, or fellowship, of the Holy Spirit* If there be any such thing as partaking with others in the possession of the Holy Spirit of God. This is that *Communion of Saints* in which we express our belief in the Apostles' Creed It is the doctrine, or let me rather say the fact, that all true Christians partake in the presence, the help and the comfort of one and the same Holy Spirit, and are thus united one to another in a degree and in a sense in which no two persons can otherwise be united, namely by being occupied and animated

[1] 2 Cor xiii 14.

by the same indwelling Spirit. I beseech you by that participation which you all have as Christians in the holy and blessed and life-giving Spirit of Christ and of God.

And, fourthly, if *any tenderness and compassions.* The former of these words is often found in Scripture; and its literal translation, as given in our Authorized Version, ill conveys its sense. It rather corresponds to our word *heart;* as when we say, Such a man has a warm heart; or, Such a man has no heart. It expresses feeling, kindness, sympathy, tenderness I beseech you then by all those tender and compassionate feelings which Christ teaches, which the Holy Spirit inspires; by all that readiness and sincerity of kindness and mercy which characterizes those who are Christians indeed, that ye rise to that effort of spiritual vigour to which I am about now to summon you.

Fulfil my joy[1]. As if he had said, I am happy, I am peaceful, I am joyful; joyful even in anxiety and suffering: but there is room for just one grain more to fill my store to overflowing; there is just one thing which you can do to make my cup of happiness run over[2]; and that is *that ye be of the same mind;* more exactly, *that ye be identically minded;* that ye have the very same thing for your mind, for your sentiment, for your thought and for your feeling. And

[1] *Verse* 2.   [2] Ps. xxiii 5

he repeats the words in three other forms, in what may be called the redundancy, the tautology of earnestness. *Having the same love;* all animated by one common and equal affection towards each other. *Of one soul;* having your very souls akin, allied, conformed, to each other. *Of one mind;* having one and the selfsame thing for the sentiment, the thought and feeling, of all and of each. It is the strongest possible description of union, of unity, as it ought to be in a Christian body.

Not at all according to, on a principle of, *partyspirit, nor according to*, under the dictates of, *vainglory; but in your humility counting each other superior to yourselves*[1]: *not regarding, each of you*—or, more exactly, *each set of you*, each little section into which you may happen to be split up by birth or circumstances, by choice or accident—*not regarding, each of you, your own things*, your own inclinations or your own interests, *but, each of you, also the things of others*[2], the inclinations and the interests, the happiness and the good, of other persons, not yourselves

The great importance of the subject thus presented constrains me to turn at once to its direct enforcement and personal application. The subject itself is that of Christian unity : and the context gives us also, first, its conditions, and secondly, its motives.

1. *Fulfil ye my joy, that ye be of one mind* St

[1] *Verse* 3.   [2] *Verse* 4.

Paul's happiness was not quite complete, until he could see those whom he loved, as he loved these Philippians, walking in unity. Where is the congregation now which can be said to be, as a body, living in unity? Is it true of this congregation, that it is a united, a sympathizing, and a loving body?

There may be unity without acquaintance; and there may be unity amidst variety. These two defects (as they might appear) are not fatal to the unity of which St Paul speaks. In every large community there must be many who know not each other by intercourse, by sight, by name: they may be united for all that. Again, in our days there are varieties in the mode and form of worship. There are those who do not value as we value, nor judge as we judge of our own Church ordinances and Church Liturgy: we regret it; we wish it were otherwise; we hope it may be otherwise some day with some of them: but we can go so far as to hope that real unity, the unity which St Paul here enforces, need not be destroyed by this diversity: we hope that we may still walk in love even with those who differ from us about Church government or Church doctrine: and we feel that strong language about the sin of schism may sometimes itself be guilty of the very sin which it condemns. It may be one art of our watchful and subtle adversary to divert our attention from real to fancied dangers, and to make us, in our zeal for a desirable but unattainable unity of form, overlook a far more desirable and perhaps not utterly hopeless unity of spirit.

No, my brethren, these things are not the real, certainly not the most formidable impediments to Christian unity: its worst dangers lie nearer to us than these. St Paul here shews us what they are. He points out what I have called the conditions of unity: and they are two: humility, and unselfishness.

i. Humility *Act not*, he says, *on a principle of party-spirit or of vainglory · but in your humility count each other superior to yourselves.* Yes, vanity, and the attendant here assigned to it, party-spirit, the love of making and (if possible) of heading parties, parties in religion, or parties in politics, or, more often still, parties in society, cliques to which we confine all our civilities and all our hospitalities, and from which we rigidly exclude all that we deem vulgar or inferior, but not always all that we ought to deem unchristian or immoral or scandalous; these things, far more than conscientious dissent whether in worship or doctrine, are the true enemies of our unity and concord, and he who would be a Christian indeed, in St Paul's sense of the term, must beware yet more of these than of that. There is but one way of excluding them from our own hearts: for we are all prone to them in one shape or in another, to the spirit of party and to the spirit of vanity: and that is, the cultivation, by prayer and watchfulness, of that deep and genuine humility which St Paul here describes as the really thinking each other better than ourselves. There is perhaps no virtue which has more numerous counterfeits upon earth than the virtue of humility. Many of us think themselves humble if, with every feeling of contempt or resentment strong in them towards their equals, they condescend to enter a poor man's cottage, or to recognize his wants and his distresses as those of a fellow-creature. And many of us think themselves humble, in a yet more Christian sense, if, retaining their overweening estimate of their own superior merits, they yet consent in some instance as it were to waive their rights, and forego in word or act a position to which they still think themselves entitled. Great need have we all to notice the definition here given us of this great grace. It is the thinking each other superior to ourselves. It is not merely treating others with consideration and deference, but sincerely thinking them worthy of that consideration and that deference. It is not the putting on an appearance of lowliness, which is often the very cloke of pride, nay, the very effort after admiration; but the taking of the lowest place because a deep self-knowledge has taught us that it is our due; because the consciousness of the multitude of our sins and rebellions against God shews itself readily and naturally in a deportment at once serious and lowly towards our fellow-men.

And this humility is one of the conditions of a Christian unity. Need I say how it acts in this respect? Need I point out how inseparably connected are individual vanity and collective discord? how it is the assumption, and the pushing, and the arrogance, and the expectation of undue respect and deference, on the part of individuals, which causes at least half of those piques and misunderstandings and secret heartburnings which run on at last into open dissensions and into an entire disruption, in a town and in a congregation, of the seamless coat, of the unity of the body of Christ?

ii. And thus we pass naturally to the second condition of unity, which is unselfishness. It is difficult entirely to separate unselfishness from humility. Nor is it necessary. The two graces have their root in one. *Look not each of you on your own things, but each of you also on the things of others.* Vanity is a fruitful cause of dissension: but below vanity itself lies ever a foundation of selfishness. To be selfish is to look only at our own things; our own inclination, our own pleasure, our own honour, our own interest. Alas! which of us is free from this charge? Over and above that reasonable and right concern for our own safety and well-being, which is the instinct of our nature, what an amount is there in each of us of self-seeking, self-concentration and self-love, which is no instinct, but a mere perversion, distortion and abuse of nature! Into what department of life does not our selfishness enter? Not only does it shew itself, as we might expect, in our business, in the struggle of one to outstrip another, in the grasping for extended employment and increased profit, in the thirst for mercantile success or professional distinction. not only in these things, which are its natural home and sphere, is the spirit of selfishness discernible: it is found also in our charity, and it is found also in our religion. In the one it shews itself in self-will, in ostentation, in self-complacency, in large demands for gratitude, in a quickness to take offence, to condemn and to despair: in the other, it shews itself in a morbid anxiety about our own personal good, in a weighing and measuring all things by their influence upon our own spiritual comfort, in a narrowness and coldness of interest in the spread of Christ's Gospel and in the advancement of God's glory. These things of themselves indicate a disregard of Christian unity as a definite object and as a constraining motive. Even these things are fatal to that oneness of heart and soul which is St Paul's definition of true communion : how much more those lower and yet commoner workings of the selfish spirit, in things altogether of time and of the world, which tend directly towards strife and discord, and are as hostile to social happiness as to the spiritual life.

Fulfil ye my joy, that ye be of one mind, of one soul.

Set it before yourselves as a high and glorious object, that we of this place be not only individually Christian but collectively united. Perfect peace indeed there will not be until the last enemy has been destroyed and sin itself is cast into the lake of fire. But even an approach to unity is blessed. Even a struggle after unity has God's mark upon it, and shall in no wise lose its reward. In every indication here given of a concern for others, in every offering cast here into the treasury of God for a humane or Christian purpose; in every effort made by any one of you to conquer selfishness in the cause of charity, to forego inclination, comfort, or ease, that you may teach the ignorant, visit the sick, or promote the heartiness of the Church's worship, in each one of these things we see a consciousness, greatly to be valued, of the meaning and of the importance of unity we see you recognizing a wider sphere of duty and a nobler object of life than that of self only. we see a foretaste at least of that coming glory when none shall think himself of any moment save in so far as he can be an instrument of good, when all things else shall be so merged and swallowed up in Christ, that He alone shall be thought of, He alone served, He alone honoured, throughout the universe of His creation, throughout the eternity of His reign.

2. Now therefore, in conclusion, we will briefly remind ourselves of the motives by which Christian

unity is here recommended and enforced. *I beseech you*, St Paul says in effect, *by every comfort and by every privilege of the Gospel*. If there be any such thing as consolation in Christ, if there be any such thing as comfort in love, if any such thing as a joint participation in the Holy Spirit, if any such thing as a heart of pitying compassion, then by all these things I beseech you to be of one soul and of one mind If you know nothing of any one of these things, then indeed I cannot hope to move you. But then also I must warn you that you are not Christians. If you are Christians, you must know something, however little, of consolation found in Christ, and of fellowship one with another in the Holy Spirit. If you are Christians, you must know something of the comfort of a true mutual love, and of that spirit of tender compassion which more than any other attribute marks out those who are heirs of heaven. I have no hope of winning you to Christian unity by an exhibition of the terrors of the Lord: *for love's sake I rather beseech you*[1]. Not to earn a place in heaven, but because you are already citizens of a heavenly city, I bid you to put away *all bitterness, and wrath, and anger, and clamour, and evil-speaking, with all malice,* and to become *kind one to another, tender-hearted, forgiving one another, even as God for Christ's sake hath forgiven you*[2]. O if there be one here pre-

---

[1] Philem 9.   [2] Eph. iv 31.

sent who feels that he is a hindrance to the unity of the Christian body; feels, in other words, that he is a proud man, or else a selfish man; feels that he is thinking of himself more highly than he ought to think[1], or looking too much at his own interests and too little upon those of others; let him ask of God a better mind: let him confess his wickedness and be sorry for his sin[2]: let him begin by plucking up from the ground of his heart this one root of bitterness[3], and asking God to sow in him in its stead that good seed in a good soil, the produce of which is unto life eternal. O, my brethren, we are not united as we ought to be. Selfish interests keep us asunder: we go each on our own way, and think little of the bodily, still less of the spiritual welfare of each other and of all. No Christian life can be vigorous where it has to be lived all alone: let us come forth out of ourselves, and look upon the work which has to be done if this world or this place is ever really to become a kingdom of our Lord and of His Christ[4]. And even if we see not in what way we can help that great, that glorious consummation—although indeed there are machineries enough at work amongst us, were there but the will to set the hand to them—yet even if we see not how, let us admit, let us feel the duty of doing something every one of us to promote Christ's glory

[1] Rom. xii. 3 [2] Ps. xxxviii. 18. [3] Heb. xii. 15.
[4] Rev. xi 15.

and to advance the good of man. He will open a door to us[1], if we are ready to enter in. And in doing anything—anything really, anything heartily, with an unselfish, a self-renouncing, self-forgetting motive—in doing anything truly for God, truly for man, without one side-look or one crooked aim at our own interest, or our own credit, or our own advantage —in doing any one such thing there is a present and a conscious as well as a prospective blessing. God's recompences are not all future: He rewards best of all by *giving more grace*[2]. *Be perfect, be of good comfort, be of one mind, live in peace; and the God of love and peace shall be with you*[3].

[1] Rev iii. 8.   [2] James iv. 6.   [3] 2 Cor xiii. 11.

SECOND SUNDAY IN ADVENT,
December 8, 1861.

LECTURE VII.

PHILIPPIANS II. 5—11.

5 L&T this mind be in you, which was also in Christ Jesus;
6 who, being originally in the form of God, thought it not a
7 thing to be seized[1] to be (exist) equally with God, but made
   Himself empty, taking the form of a servant, becoming in the
8 likeness of men; and being found in fashion as a man, He
   humbled Himself, becoming obedient, unto death, and the death
9 of the cross. Wherefore also God highly exalted Him, and
10 granted Him a name, that which is above every name, that
   in the name of Jesus every knee might bend, of beings in
11 heaven and on earth and under the earth, and every tongue
   tell out its acknowledgments that Jesus Christ is Lord, to the
   glory of God the Father.

[1] This or a kindred phrase is used by some late Greek writers in the sense of *regarding a thing as a fortunate chance, a gain or prize.*

LECTURE VII.[1]

PHILIPPIANS II. 10.

That at the name of Jesus every knee should bow

CHRISTIAN unity, its nature and importance, its conditions and its motives, formed the last subject of our meditations upon this Epistle Of its conditions the one was humility and the other unselfishness. *In lowliness of mind let each esteem other better than themselves. Look not each of you on your own things, but each of you also on the things of others*[2]. That is the connection in which the passage now before us stands. The charge to be unselfish is illustrated and enforced by the highest of all examples. *Let this mind be in you, which was also in Christ Jesus*[3].

I need not say one word to bespeak your earnest and reverent attention to the remarkable passage thus

[1] A Collection was made on this occasion in aid of the Society for the Propagation of the Gospel in Foreign Parts.
[2] Phil. II. 3, 4.   [3] *Verse* 5.

introduced. There will be something to explain in it, more to ponder. It will be found to embody just that doctrine which is most appropriate to the holy season which we are now celebrating—the commemoration of the first Advent, the anticipation of the second—and also to lay the most substantial basis for that work of faith and charity which I have undertaken to urge upon you this day.

The general subject is the unselfishness of Christ. Let that unselfish, that self-devoting, self-forgetting spirit be yours also. But here the unselfishness of Christ is drawn out for us into something of detail. We are told in what it consisted. We are taught to reflect upon what He was originally, and upon what He became for us. We are taught to observe not the fact only, but the steps and stages of His humiliation. And then we are taught to notice the reparation and reversal of that marvellous self-sacrifice; to view the greatness to which He who once suffered and died has been exalted, and the purpose of God concerning His universal rule. Let us set ourselves to this contemplation with some sense, by God's mercy, of its majesty and of its glory.

We are to take into view the following particulars. First, the original position of our Lord and Saviour Jesus Christ. Next, his humiliation, and the stages of it. Thirdly, His consequent exaltation, and the object of it. Then we shall be able to enter with more intelligence, and, I trust, with more docility also, into the exhortation which prefaces the whole description. *Let this mind be in you, which was also in Christ Jesus.*

Who, being in the form of God[1]. The exact expression is, *being originally, being to begin with, being from the first, in the form of God.* It is the very language of the opening of St John's Gospel. *In the beginning was the Word, and the Word was with God, and the Word was God*[2]. It is the very language of the opening of the Epistle to the Hebrews. *Who, being the brightness of His glory and the express image of His person*[3]. or, more exactly, *the effulgence of God's glory, and the impress of His essence.* Jesus Christ was, before He was born, was originally; was in the beginning; was from eternity; was with God, was *the image of the invisible God*[4], was the impress of God's essence; yea, Himself, as St John expressly declares, *was God.* God give us grace to accept in simplicity and to hold fast in reverence the revelation of our Lord's pre-existence, of His eternity, of His Divinity, of His oneness with God. *I and my Father are one*[5]. Such a Saviour, and such only, *became us*[6].

Being originally in the form of God, He thought it not robbery to be equal with God; to have, as it might be more exactly rendered, *equality of being with God* We have reached a very difficult expression. The

[1] *Verse* 6. [2] John i. 1. [3] Heb. i. 3.
[4] Col. i. 15. [5] John x. 30. [6] Heb. vii 26.

word rendered *robbery* is a very peculiar one. It occurs nowhere else in Scripture. In its exact form it is an unusual word everywhere. But its meaning is clearly proved by such instances as can be collected. It denotes, first, a *snatching* or *seizing;* and then, *a thing worth snatching* or *seizing*, a thing to be caught at with avidity and clung to with tenacity. And thus the words now under consideration will become, *Who, being originally in the form of God, thought it not a thing to be seized*, a thing to be grasped and clung to, *to have equality of being with God, but made Himself of no reputation*[1]—*made Himself empty* is the exact phrase —*taking the form of a servant*, that is, of a created being, *becoming in the likeness of men*. It is the first clause of the description of Christ's humiliation, that He thought not equality with God a thing to be tenaciously and selfishly clung to, if by laying it aside, by divesting Himself of it, He could redeem and save ruined man.

This was the first stage of the humiliation; the Incarnation and the Nativity; the condescension of the Creator to the likeness of created man; and not to his likeness only, but to a real participation in the human nature in both its parts, a mortal body and a finite soul.

And being found in fashion as a man[2], this first step having been taken in the valley of humiliation, *He*

[1] *Verse* 7.   [2] *Verse* 8

humbled Himself yet lower; stopped not short at the threshold of humanity, taking indeed our nature, but taking it under circumstances and conditions which might have mitigated to the utmost extent the severity of the condescension; no, *He humbled Himself by becoming obedient*, perfectly submissive to God's will, and perfectly passive in God's hands, *unto death*, to the extent even of dying in human nature—*and* what death? even *the death of the cross;* the death of the most abject, the death of the most criminal, the death on which a curse rested[1], and which made Him a very offence and stumblingblock[2] to His own to whom He came[3]. What brief, what majestic, what thrilling words! *He humbled Himself, and became obedient, unto death, even the death of the cross.*

Wherefore God also highly exalted Him, and granted Him a name, that which is above every name[4]. *Raised Him up from the dead*, St Peter writes, *and gave Him glory*[5]. *We see Jesus*, thus we read in the Epistle to the Hebrews, *who was made a little lower than the angels for the suffering of death, crowned with glory and honour*[6]. The *name given* here is the *glory and honour* there. *That in the name of Jesus every knee might bend, of beings in heaven and on earth and under the earth*[7], that is, of all God's creatures,

[1] Deut. xxi. 23; Gal. iii. 13. [2] 1 Cor i. 23
[3] John i 11. [4] *Verse* 9. [5] 1 Pet. 1. 21.
[6] Heb. ii. 9. [7] *Verse* 10.

whether angelic or human, whether living or dead, *and every tongue tell out its acknowledgments that Jesus Christ is Lord, to the glory of God the Father*[1]. Where Christ is honoured, God is honoured[2]. There can be no separation of interests there. Whatever exalts Christ glorifies God. *Who by Him (Christ) do believe in God, that raised Him up from the dead and gave Him glory, that your faith and hope might be in God*[3].

That in the name of Jesus every knee might bend. The bending of the knee is sometimes the act of homage. *As I live, saith the Lord, every knee shall bow to me, and every tongue shall confess to God*[4]. Sometimes it is an act of worship. *For this cause I bow my knees unto the Father of our Lord Jesus Christ, of whom the whole family in heaven and earth is named, that He would grant you*[5], &c. In this latter sense the expression appears to be used in the text. *That in the name of Jesus every knee may bend.* That, whenever and wherever prayer is offered, it may be offered in the name of Jesus, on the ground of what He has done, and in dependence upon His mediation and intercession. The other act, that of homage, is expressed in the words which follow; *and that every tongue may confess that Jesus Christ is Lord.*

These then are stated as the two objects of the

---

[1] *Verse* 11.   [2] John v 23.   [3] 1 Pet. 1 21.
[4] Isai xlv. 23, Rom. xiv. 11.   [5] Eph iii 14, 15.

exaltation, after humiliation, of our Lord and Saviour. First, that all God's creatures may worship in His name. And, secondly, that all God's creatures may confess and avow His rule. Is not this a Missionary subject? Could I have found a topic more exactly suitable to a call to assist in propagating Christ's Gospel?

1. *That in the name of Jesus every knee may bend.* Even Angels are to worship in the name of Jesus. It is more to the purpose for us to remember that God desires men, all men, so to worship. And it is a thought at once solemnizing and comforting, that not only living men, but the dead also, are required to call upon God in the name of Jesus.

It is assumed in the words of the text that all God's creatures will bend the knee somehow. Prayer is an instinct of nature. God has so made us, that we feel a power above us, and desire that that power should be friendly to us and not hostile. The first element of prayer is the calling in of that power, the praying it not to be unfriendly to us, not to exert itself to crush, but to benefit, to bless, to save. The poor idolater does that. All his miserable superstitions point that way. O Thou who hast power over me, bless and curse not! And lest after all his guessings and all his outcries he should at last misapprehend or miscall the right object of this supplication, he has been known to add to all the other deities with which he has crowded his Pantheon, an altar bearing this inscription, *To the*

Unknown God[1]. O Thou who hast power over me, if I have thus far missed Thee, if I have not yet paid Thee the becoming homage, accept, I pray, this anonymous offering, and even under the title of the Unknown God be my Benefactor and my Protector! Surely there is something, even in these vaguest cries, plaintive and pitiable in the air of humanity. Surely he who comes even to such a people, with a mind taught of God and a heart softened by His Spirit, will find no terms of reproach or insult with which to open his ministrations, but will say rather, in the very words of his inspired prototype St Paul, *Whom therefore ye ignorantly worship, Him declare I unto you.*

Prayer, in some form, is an instinct But how is it with the prayer spoken of in the text? Is prayer in the name of Jesus an instinct? Is it the prayer which even Christians always offer? Are there none, none even in this congregation, who bend the knee, if indeed they do bend it, rather in their own name than in His? To pray in the name of Jesus is to pray as persons whom He has authorized to pray; persons whom He has desired to use His name with God; to say, I come because of Jesus Christ, because of His humiliation and because of His exaltation, because He suffered and died for me, because He rose again and lives again for me. That is the name which is our passport: that is the

[1] Acts xvii 23.

name which *has power with God and prevails*[1]*:* that is
the name which we must take with us if we would
know what it is to be heard and to be answered. Let
us pray always in the name of Jesus: not in our own
name ; not as though our claim were anything, or as
though our wish had any right to be gratified ; not as
though there were something acceptable in our con-
descending to recognize God as the Giver of all good
or the Protector in all dangers; but in the name of
Jesus: not only remembering to add His name at
the end of our prayers, and say, as our Church ever
teaches us to say, *through Jesus Christ our Lord...
through our only Mediator and Advocate Jesus Christ;*
but also relying throughout upon His work of redemption and upon His word of promise; praying on the
strength of Christ ; as those whom He has redeemed ;
as those to whom He has given access; as those to
whom He has given His credentials, so that we have
boldness to enter into the holiest by the blood of Jesus[2].
That in the name of Jesus every knee may bend. Let us
earnestly ask of God the grace so to approach Him.

2. *And that every tongue may confess that Jesus
Christ is Lord.* This is the second part of the design
of the exaltation of Jesus. God will have Him owned
as Lord throughout the whole world. Yes, the praises
of the Church, as well as the prayers of the Church,
have a value in heaven. Wherever the sound is heard

[1] Gen. xxxii 28. [2] Heb. x 19.

from believing hearts and from adoring lips, *Thou art the King of glory, O Christ*, there is a sound acceptable to God. *Day by day we magnify Thee: and we worship Thy Name ever world without end.* We do not think enough of these things If God exalted Jesus when He had first stooped to death and the grave, it was with a definite purpose, one part of which was that every tongue might tell out its acknowledgments that Jesus Christ is Lord. That is a confession which ever redounds, as it is here written, *to the glory of God the Father*.

Learn, my brethren, to think more of the work of acknowledging Jesus as that which He indeed is, God's Lord and God's Christ[1]. The religion of many Christians never gets beyond prayer. There is not a word of praise in it. There is no bold, frank, honest avowal of convictions deeply cherished as to the Person and as to the work of Christ. When they come together to worship, they take but a feeble and languid interest in those parts of the service—and they are many—in which nothing is asked, in which God is only adored, in which Christ is only magnified. *We praise Thee, O God: we acknowledge Thee to be the Lord...Glory be to the Father, and to the Son, and to the Holy Ghost: As it was in the beginning, is now, and ever shall be, world without end.*

And need I say that such language in God's wor-

[1] Acts ii. 36; iv. 26.

ship ought to be consistent with the still more real language of the life? *Why call ye me, Lord, Lord*, our Saviour Himself asks of us, *and do not the things which I say*[1]*?* If the tongue confesses that Jesus Christ is Lord, ought not our acts and common words, our habits and principles, our aims and our motives, to say the same thing; to shew that we own His dominion, that we feel ourselves to be His servants and His subjects? The acknowledgment which is frank and emphatic ought to be consistent also and harmonious.

These are vague words: words soon uttered; words sure to be accepted, while they speak but to the crowd. If they were spoken to us one by one, they would be heard impatiently by some, angrily by some, timidly, sadly, sorrowfully by more Whose life would bear comparison with his creed? Who would not be accused and condemned if what he says here concerning Christ were repeated to him, with close questioning, in his life of business or in his life at home?

To-day I would ask you to do something in consequence of your faith in Christ. You have heard that it is God's will that all prayer should be made in the name of Jesus, and that every tongue should confess that He is Lord. If you yourself believe in Him as your Saviour, you must desire that it should be so. You must desire that a growing number, at last that all mankind, should learn to pray through Christ, and

[1] Luke vi. 46.

should learn to confess Christ. You know that that is the consummation for which we pray, as often as we utter the familiar words, *Thy kingdom come*[1]. Every little effort that we can make here around us has this end in view. We desire to be instrumental in bringing some who now pray not, or pray as it were in their own name, to bend their knee in the name of Jesus. We desire to be instrumental in bringing some who now acknowledge no sovereignty but that of self and sin, to confess in heart, in tongue, and in life, that Jesus Christ is Lord. I hope and believe that there are many in this congregation whose hearts testify within them that this is their desire, this their aim, this, in some small degree, their endeavour. Will these listen unmoved to a call which summons them to wider action, and bids them remember those whose only chance (humanly speaking) of ever hearing the name of Jesus, of ever praying through Him or ever praising Him, lies in the operation of such machinery as that which is to-day waiting your aid?

Let this mind be in you, which was also in Christ Jesus. He whom you are now bidden to confess as your Lord and your God, was once in glory and in blessedness, and He divested Himself of both for you. He came on earth, as at this season, to be born in human nature, and to learn obedience by the things which He suffered. *Unto death, even the death of the*

[1] Matt. vi 10; Luke xi. 2.

cross—thus far did He carry His obedience and His sacrifice. He utterly disregarded, refused and forgot self, that He might be and that He might do for others that which they could not do and could not be for themselves. Not in vain surely will this example be set forth to us. Great things indeed we are not asked to do in imitation of it. Well may we feel ourselves humbled when we compare our best charities, our highest unselfishnesses, with those of the Incarnation and of the Cross But let us not therefore neglect to do what we can. If the thing itself to which we are called is poor and mean; the gift of a small offering of perishable money, of sincere sympathy, or of hearty prayer; still let the motive, let the spirit ennoble it. Emulate the mind which was in Christ Jesus: then will the deed done be raised and consecrated by it. Let Him who seeth in secret[1] behold a true faith and fervent love; yea, let Him, even as He is willing, awaken that faith and kindle that love by the presence within us of His Holy Spirit; and doubt not that He will both accept the offering, and also prosper it, by almighty power, in the work to which you give it.

[1] Matt. vi. 4, 6, 18.

THIRD SUNDAY IN ADVENT,
December 15, 1861.

LECTURE VIII.

PHILIPPIANS II. 12, 13.

12   W<small>HEREFORE</small>, *my beloved, as ye always obeyed, not as in my presence only, but now much more in my absence, work*
13 *out your own salvation with fear and trembling: for it is God who worketh in you both the willing and the working, in behalf of His good pleasure.*

LECTURE VIII.

PHILIPPIANS II. 12, 13

*Work out your own salvation with fear and trembling:
for it is God which worketh in you.*

THESE, you will all say, are among the most weighty words in all Scripture. They consist of a charge, and a reason for it. They put together two great doctrines, often held to be incompatible, and boldly connect them with the word *for*. There is much in each of the doctrines by itself: there is more in their combination: there is more still in the mode of their combination. Upon each of these topics I propose to address a few plain words to my friends and hearers this morning— the last Sunday morning of an expiring year. Let that reflection add weight, if it be possible, to the text itself; add seriousness, at all events, to the hearts that listen!

We will first regard the two clauses of the text separately: we will then combine them. And may the topics presented, as they are certainly important and certainly seasonable, so be also made interesting to you, and by God's grace fruitful too!

1. *Work out your own salvation with fear and trembling.* The charge is introduced in connection with that subject which last occupied us on a similar occasion, the humiliation and exaltation of Christ, and the purpose of that glory after suffering. Be not selfish, St Paul had said. Think of Christ. Think what He was originally, and think what He became, and what He did, and what He suffered, for you: and let the mind which was in Him be in you also. He left His eternal glory: He took upon Him the form of a creature: He humbled Himself, He became obedient, unto death, the death of the cross: from that lowest deep of humiliation God exalted Him, gave Him a name above every name, a name in which every created being shall worship, a name which every tongue shall confess. *Wherefore, my beloved,* seeing that these things are so, seeing that Christ thus humbled Himself and was afterwards thus exalted, assured that these mighty and marvellous events were not for nothing, assured that there must have been a fearful necessity for that humiliation, and that there must be a fearful urgency of consequences from that exaltation, I charge you, *as ye always obeyed,* from the first day that you received the truth, so, *not as in my presence only,* not as though it were only while I was with you that the call of the Gospel was persuasive, *but now much more*

in my absence, when more is thrown upon you, when your own personal faithfulness is more severely tried, *work out,* accomplish, work so as to succeed in working, *your own salvation with fear and trembling*[1].

So then there is a sense in which salvation is not yet wrought out, not yet accomplished, not yet wrought so as to be wrought successfully. St Paul says that the Philippians had still thus to work out their own salvation. And yet to the Ephesians he says, *By grace,* by God's free and unmerited favour, *ye are (have been) saved*[2], already saved. And to the Romans, *We are (were) saved by hope*[3] And to Timothy he speaks of *the power of God who saved us*[4], as though it were a past thing The connecting link between the two expressions, between his speaking of salvation as already accomplished and his speaking of salvation as a thing still to be accomplished, is found in such passages as those in which he speaks to the Corinthians of the proclamation of the Cross as being *to us who are (being) saved the power of God*[5], and again of the Gospel as the means *by which also ye are (being) saved*[6], are in course and process of salvation.

These are, both and all, true sayings. The Christian is saved. Christ has borne his sins[7]: Christ has done all for him[8]; Christ is his sufficient sacrifice[9],

[1] *Verse* 12. [2] Eph ii. 5. [3] Rom viii 24.
[4] 2 Tim 1 9 [5] 1 Cor. 1 18 [6] chap. xv 2
[7] 1 Pet ii 24 [8] Col. ii. 10. [9] John i. 29.

Christ is his availing Intercessor[1], Christ is charged with his soul[2], Christ is already his life[3], and because Christ lives, he lives also[4]. But yet, though saved, he is not safe: though all has been done for him, he is not in repose: though his true life is hidden with Christ in God, yet his lower life is still lived on earth, in a world of abounding temptation, of perpetual turmoil, of overflowing iniquity, of unrest therefore, of anxiety, yes, of risk. Like St Peter walking upon the water[5] he is safe while he looks to Christ, but he is not safe from the danger of looking off from Christ. If he does that, he begins to sink. If he does not then speedily recover himself by crying, *Lord, save me*, he will go on sinking —he may sink deep—yes, my brethren, it is idle to deny it, he may go down. The elect are safe: but who are they? Who, save in a retrospect which can be taken individually only from heaven, will dare to say of himself positively, I am one of the elect: I know therefore that I can never fall? Perseverance is a privilege of the elect: but what sign is there of the elect, what infallible sign, save perseverance? *He that shall endure unto the end, the same shall be saved*[6]*:* till that endurance is completed, who shall presume upon it?

The Christian has been saved, is being saved; still has to be saved. The three expressions are equally

---

[1] Heb. vii 25. [2] 2 Tim i. 12 [3] Col. iii. 4.
[4] John xiv 19. [5] Matt xiv 28—31.
[6] Matt xxiv 13, Mark xiii 13

just, for they are equally Scriptural. The Ephesians had been already saved by grace. The Corinthians were being saved by means of the Gospel. The Philippians had still to go on working out their salvation And yet no difference is thus put between the spiritual advancement of the three congregations. Of the three perhaps the Philippians were in the most advanced condition. And yet they are charged to work out their salvation; and that, with fear and trembling. My brethren, it is no mark of great attainments in faith, and it is no characteristic of what ought to be meant by the words *high doctrine*, to refuse and repudiate this condition. We may be well contented if we are as far advanced as the Philippians here addressed, or if our theology is as sound as that of St Paul who here addresses them. We shall find hereafter that St Paul accepted for himself the very same position, in this respect, as that which he assigns to them[1]. He was still working out his salvation with fear and trembling.

But is there then no such thing as Christian confidence, Christian peace, or Christian joy? Is a Christian man, is a Christian woman, to be a person living in a perpetual depression, in a fever of spiritual anxiety, in a palsy of religious trembling? We would say again, Look at these Philippians. Look at St Paul. Who was ever a more bold, a more trusting, a more hopeful, yes, a more joyful man? The Christian

[1] Phil. iii. 12.

state, with him, was, as it always ought to be, a compound state. It is a condition made up of various, of opposite ingredients. There is sorrow for sin: there is peace in believing. There is the fear of God: there is the love of God. There is the sense of weakness: there is the consciousness of strength. There is salvation rejoiced in · there is salvation to be wrought out Never was the contrast more forcibly stated than by St Paul himself. *As dying, and, behold, we live; as chastened, and not killed; as sorrowful, yet alway rejoicing, as poor, yet making many rich; as having nothing, and yet possessing all things*[1]. When the Christian rejoices, he rejoices in the Lord: when he fears, he fears himself. If he stands fast, he shall be saved, yes, is saved already: he trembles only lest he should not stand fast. And even there, he doubts not the will and the power of God to hold him up, to keep him stedfast; he only fears, as his own holy Scriptures, as his own Saviour and His Apostles, teach him to do, lest at any time his heart should be overcharged with worldly indulgences or worldly cares[2], lest any insidious root of bitterness should spring up to trouble and defile him[3], lest his spiritual adversary, *seeking whom he may devour*[4], should tempt him unawares, should beguile him from his God, and so his labour be in vain[5] and he find himself ashamed

---

[1] 2 Cor. vi. 9, 10. [2] Luke xxi. 34 [3] Heb. xii. 15.
[4] 1 Pet v. 8. [5] 1 Thess iii.

before Christ at His coming[1]. On these accounts he listens, while he may, to the warning voice of the Apostle, when it bids him not to be highminded, but to fear[2]; not to presume, but to watch and pray[3]; not to count himself to have attained, but to be ever working out his salvation with fear and trembling.

2. Let us now turn to the opposite half of the text. A Christian must work out his own salvation: that is one truth. It is God who works in him both to will and to do: that is the other truth. Two things, contrary indeed, but not contradictory: or, if contradictory, yet only so to that logical faculty in man, which has its place in things of the dry cold intellect, but which has no place in things of the higher reason, of the conscience, and of the soul.

It is God who worketh in you both the willing and the working, in behalf of, and so, to effect, to bring about, *His good pleasure*[4]; His gracious will, of which Christ and His Apostles speak so often, that you should be saved. *This is the will of God, even your sanctification*[5]. *God will have all men to be saved*[6].

Now observe the fulness and the strength of the expressions here used. Most men are ready to acknowledge that they must have God's concurrence, in order to do what is right. They need the assistance of His Providence, they say; not only to pre-

---

[1] 1 John ii 28. [2] Rom. xi. 20. [3] Matt. xxvi. 41.
[4] *Verse* 13. [5] 1 Thess. iv 3. [6] 1 Tim. ii 4.

serve life, and to make action of any kind possible; but also, in some undefined manner, to assist and cooperate with their good endeavours. And some men —most men, perhaps, in doctrine and theory—go further, and say that they need God's grace to enable them to carry into act their good desires and resolutions. Would to God, my brethren, that all of us had got even thus far in the personal knowledge of the truth! For then surely there would be a large accession to the number of those who pray; a larger accession still to the frequency, the earnestness and the minuteness of their prayers. If indeed it is God who works in us to do—to execute our purposes, to turn wishes into resolutions, and resolutions into efforts, and efforts into successes—there is wide scope for prayer, and no little peril in omitting or trifling with it.

But what shall we say, when the Apostle here goes further, and tells us that it is God who works in us even to will? that there is not a holy desire, not a good counsel, any more than there can be a just work, which does not proceed from Him, which does not originate in Him[1]? that it is He who prevents as well as follows us in all our doings, and not only furthers us with His continual help[2], but also sets us from the first moment in the way of His steps[3]? Go back as

---

[1] Second Collect at Evening Prayer.
[2] Fourth Collect after the Offertory.   [3] Ps. lxxxv. 13.

far as we may into the origination of our acts, we can never find the point at which God was not present, at which God was not engaged, in the production of any one action which was at all right and good. It is He who is the Author of good, in each single instance of conduct, as well as in the formation of character or the shaping of a life. As it is with the salvation of a soul, that in all true doctrine the final result is referred back to God's fore-knowledge and God's predestination and God's calling[1], while the fullest scope is given to man's free agency and to man's free will[2], so is it with the separate acts of such as shall be saved: in them, that is, in their fallen nature, dwells no good thing[3]: whatever is good in them, if it be but in wish, in desire, in will, is entirely of God: left to themselves, they could no more purpose right than do it: it is God who worketh in them both to will and to do of His good pleasure.

The inference from this part of the truth is clear and decisive. He who would do right, he therefore who would will right, must be in constant communication with God; must have God's hand, which is God's Spirit, continually with him, touching the inmost spring of being, and thus setting in motion every complex wheel of the spiritual life. If you are not much with God—seeking Him, communing with

[1] Rom. viii. 29, 30. [2] John v. 40; Rev. xxii. 17.
[3] Rom. vii 18.

Him, receiving of that living water[1] which is the Holy Spirit of Christ, by means of prayer which is the appointed means of drawing it from its deep and secret well—if this is not your life, the life of your soul within, the life of your weekday as well as of your Sunday, you cannot be in the right way to heaven. I know that there is a mystery in all this; a mystery not easy to read; a mystery which in this world will never be done away: and I know that there are many hindrances, many interruptions, many impediments, to this life of Divine intercourse and communion: we can feel for one another, and feel with one another, as to the difficulties which beset our path and the shadows which lie heavily upon our goal: but still let us, as the Holy Spirit teaches us, rather *provoke one another*[2] to this life, than encourage ourselves or others in despairing of it: let us say to ourselves—and God grant that the words may sound in other ears beside our own this day—If it is God who works in Christians both to will and to do, to Him will I seek, for Him will I wait, with Him will I abide, day by day, that He may both lay in me the train of holy resolution, and also kindle it into action by the spark of His grace.

3. And now, in the third and last place, we will endeavour to combine, after St Paul's example, these two halves of the Divine truth. Many teachers would

[1] John iv. 10—14.   [2] Heb. x. 24.

have said, for many teachers say in effect now, *Work out your own salvation with fear and trembling*, though indeed *it is God*—or, but remember *it is God—who worketh in you*. Not so the inspired guide who goes before us in the text. He, in the full assurance of faith, has written the words, *Work out your own salvation…*for *it is God who worketh in you* Work out your own salvation, just because the power to do so is not your own. *Work out your own salvation with fear and trembling*, not though, but *because it is God who worketh in you both to will and to do of His good pleasure*.

And we may see two reasons, different but harmonious, for this connection.

i First, a motive of warning Like the high priest, admitted, under the Old Testament dispensation, once a year into the most holy place which was a type of God's immediate presence[1], you must be careful how you exercise a privilege so awful, a right so responsible You know with what care and fear, with what ablutions and purifications, in what sacred vestments and with what passports of sacrificial blood, the priest of God made his way, on that solemn anniversary, into a presence-chamber locked otherwise against the living: think whether you can pass your life, as Christians do, in a place holier than the most holy, a temple not made with hands, but spiritual and

---

[1] Lev. xvi. 2, &c.; Heb. ix. 7, 8.

eternal, even that heaven where Christ sitteth at the right hand of God[1]—think whether you can yourself be one of God's temples[2], with the Holy Ghost in you working both to will and to do of God's good pleasure —and not require, for your safety, a spirit of reverence and of circumspection, yea, a spirit even of sober and godly fear, beyond that of any minister in holy places made with hands, which at last were but figures of the true[3], the heavenly temple. Think what it must be for a man to have God so near him that his very actions, his very will, are ruled and guided by His inworking Well may he whose privilege it is to have God in him by His Holy Spirit, working both to will and to do, live and move ever as in a supernatural presence; keep his heart and watch his life with all diligence[4]; yea, even as it is written, work out his own salvation day by day with fear and trembling!

ii. Finally, and yet more directly, we have here a motive of hope. We all know something of the effects of discouragement; how it paralyzes exertion, how it even diminishes power. Say to a man, You are failing—you cannot do it—there is not a chance of your success—and can there be any result so probable as that he will fail? Say to him, Here is that which guarantees to you success; take it, use it, and

---

[1] Col. iii. 1.   [2] 1 Cor. vi. 19.
[3] Heb. ix. 24.   [4] Prov. iv 23.

you cannot fail: say to him, By this means I succeeded, and the same method is at your command: what will he not do under that stimulus? Such is the very argument here employed. *Work out your salvation with fear and trembling:* why? because you are on the brink of ruin? because you are a lost man if you relax your efforts? because hell has enlarged herself for you[1], and heaven, if won at all, can be won only by gigantic toils? Not so. but because, if you try, you will certainly succeed; because God knows your weakness[2], and will replace it by His strength[3]; knows your difficulties, and will make mountains a plain before you[4], because, feeling for you, because, desiring your good, because, loving you with an everlasting love[5], He has so arranged for you as that you cannot fail if you use His means; because, aware of the bondage of your own will to evil, He has undertaken to will in you; because, aware of the frailty of your nature, He has undertaken to act in you—on these accounts, trusting in Him who has pledged to you a Divine strength and possessed you with an Almighty Spirit, set out afresh day by day in your heavenward journey; watch and pray in your hour of temptation, resist and faint not in your season of conflict; yea, *work out your own salvation with fear and trembling*, because *it is God who worketh in you both to will and to do!*

[1] Isa. v. 14. [2] 2 Cor. xii. 9. [3] Heb. xi. 34.
[4] Zech. iv. 7. [5] Jer. xxxi. 3.

God give us all grace, my brethren, not only to admit the cogency of the inspired reasoning, but to be convinced, to be moved, to be stirred by it ourselves! God give us grace, not only to see the connection between man's helplessness and man's responsibility, not only to apprehend justly man's part and God's part in the work of salvation, but, ourselves, our own living selves—the men and the women whose souls are here trembling in the balance between eternal life and eternal death—to be aroused to decision, to a decision firm and prompt, as to the things which belong to our peace[1]! Men and brethren[2], children of the stock of Adam, taken from the earth and soon to return to it[3], yet having within you, each one, a living soul which, in happiness or else in misery, must for ever and for ever be, to you is the word of this salvation sent! *See, O see, that ye refuse not Him that speaketh[4]!*

[1] Luke xix 42
[2] Acts xiii 26.
[3] Eccles xii 7
[4] Heb. xii. 25.

FIRST SUNDAY AFTER CHRISTMAS,
    December 29, 1861

LECTURE IX.

PHILIPPIANS II. 14—16.

¹⁴₁₅ *Do all things without murmurings and disputings, that ye may become blameless and pure, children of God irreproachable amidst a crooked and perverse generation (of men) amongst* 16 *whom ye shine as lights in the world, applying a word of life; unto triumph for me against the day of Christ, because I ran not in vain nor laboured in vain.*

LECTURE IX.

PHILIPPIANS II. 16.

Holding forth the word of life.

IT is the natural sequel to that consideration of the inward life of a Christian, which occupied us last Sunday morning, to enquire what should be his aspect, and what his aim, towards those without; towards those who are either avowedly or practically living without Christ and without God in the world. This is the general subject of the brief passage now lying before us.

Do all things without murmurings and disputings[1]. *Murmurings* are secret complainings, whether against God or man: *disputings* are those debatings and wranglings which spring out of, and give expression to, the other. *That ye may become*, prove yourselves, *blameless and pure*[2]*: blameless;* not only free from reproach, but safe from reproach; not blamed, and not to be blamed,

[1] *Verse* 14 [2] *Verse* 15

persons of whom the world shall have no evil thing to say[1]: *and pure:* it is the same word which our Lord uses when He bids His disciples to be *wise as serpents, and* harmless *as doves*[2]*:* it is properly descriptive of those in whom there is no admixture; amongst whose good there is no adjunct or compound of evil it is the word which St Paul applies when he urges the Roman Christians to be *wise unto that which is good, and* simple *concerning evil*[3]

That ye may be blameless and pure, children of God irreproachable (not to be blamed) amidst a crooked and perverse generation The last words are first found in the Song of Moses in the Book of Deuteronomy. *They are a perverse and crooked generation*[4]. *Save yourselves,* St Peter said on the great day of Pentecost, *from this untoward (crooked) generation*[5]. *O faithless and perverse generation,* our Lord asked, *how long shall I be with you? how long shall I suffer you*[6]*?* This was that crookedness which had to be made straight[7], before the glory of the Lord could be revealed to man. This was that perverseness, or distortion, of the mind and of the will, which must be exchanged for directness and for uprightness, before all flesh could see the salvation of God. It was so, and it is so still. It was so in days of heathen blindness and of Jewish obstinacy: it is so in

---

[1] Tit. ii. 8 [2] Matt x. 16. [3] Rom xvi 19
[4] Deut. xxxii. 5. [5] Acts ii 40 [6] Matt. xvii 17.
[7] Isai. xl 4; Luke iii 5.

days of boasted liberality and in the heart of a nominal Christendom. There is a crookedness of the moral standard, a perverseness and distortion of the affections and the will, which, under whatever name, is the natural enemy of Christ's Gospel, and which forms a dark fringe, an impervious border, in every country and in every place, around the bright luminous body of a true devoted Christianity *Amongst whom ye shine as lights in the world* According to our Lord's well-remembered saying in the Sermon on the Mount, *Let your light so shine before men, that they may see your good works, and glorify your Father which is in heaven*[1].

Holding forth (*applying*, or *presenting*) *a word of life*[2], the message which declares to us eternal life; that Gospel by which Christ *abolishes death and brings life and immortality to light*[3]

Unto triumph for me against the day of Christ, because I ran not in vain, nor laboured in vain. that it may be seen, in the day of Christ's coming, to my joy and glory, that my earthly race was not one of disappointment or defeat, that my labour bestowed upon you was not in vain, but blessed with an abundant harvest.

Holding forth the word of life. The expression is sometimes restricted to preachers and ministers of the Gospel. But you see how evidently it has a wider range. It is addressed by the preacher to his congre-

[1] Matt. v. 16.   [2] *Verse* 16.   [3] 2 Tim 1. 10.

gation. It is a charge laid by St Paul upon Christians generally, that they hold forth the word of life, and thus shine as lights in the world, in the midst of a crooked and perverse generation. The figure is derived, we may suppose, from a person holding a light to shew the way to others: and the light so held is described as the word of life. It is the business of all Christians to use the Gospel, which is first in their own hearts, as a guiding light to others who are still included in the mass of crookedness and perverseness around We will devote our few words of Christian meditation this morning to this subject. We saw last Sunday what a Christian has to do in saving himself; what need he has to work out his own salvation even with fear and trembling[1]: and we saw what his encouragement is in endeavouring to obey this precept; namely, that he is not left to himself in doing so; it is God that worketh in him; and that, not only to do, not only to bring his good resolutions to good effect, but also to will, to suggest the holy desire, to form it into a good counsel, as well as finally to mature it into a just work. And to-day we are to add another feature to this deeply important truth: namely, that even this kind of earnest and vigorous religion has need to beware lest it should run into selfishness, selfishness of a very high and refined order, but selfishness still; the religion of one who thinks only of himself, though it be of the

[1] Phil ii. 12, 13

highest part of himself, his immortal soul, that, if a man would be a Christian indeed, he must look not only at his own things, but also at the things of others and at the things of Christ[1], how he may so present and apply the light of His Gospel, that it may penetrate here and there into the deep gloom around, and lead others, seeing his good works, to glorify, like him and with him, his Father who is in heaven.

The two things are not indeed so distinct as in words they appear to be. In the very act of working out his own salvation, if he be rightly taught what that charge means, a man will be, incidentally at least, holding forth, or applying to others, the word of life. This is true in some measure. But so prone are we all to selfishness, so prone to religious selfishness when we are driven out of that selfishness which is altogether indolent and worldly, and so many are there who would foster this spiritual selfishness by precepts distorted from the Gospel, that it is necessary to give reality and prominence to the charge before us by examining it, even as we are here taught to do, separately and in detail.

1. It is your business, my brethren, quite as much as it is our business, the special object of our ministry amongst you, to hold forth the word of life. Your work on earth is not done, when you have saved yourself from an untoward generation. You have still to hold

[1] ch. ii. 4, 21.

your lamp as far in as you can into the dark mass around. God does not call you to a timid, fugitive, skulking piety, a religion which has to lock its doors and bar its windows, that it may be alone by itself in the sight of a God who seeth in secret. There is a part of it which has to do this. To be worth anything, even for purposes of diffusion, our lamp must be kindled in secret, and fed in secret, and trimmed in secret. We can soon tell those whose religion has no such seclusion. But the office of the lamp is to shine. Men do not light a candle to put it under a bed, but to set it on a candlestick, that it may give light to all that are in the house[1]. Even so it is with the Christian's lamp, which is the word of life.

The first point is, that we be impressed, by the help of God's Holy Spirit, with the conviction that we have a duty outside of ourselves. I know that there are many of us who admit that it is pleasing and amiable and praiseworthy to seek the good of others; persons who would not read unmoved the record of Christian zeal and self-devotion going into lanes or prisons or distant lands in the hope of reclaiming the outcast, comforting the wretched, or saving the lost; but who yet look upon all these things, in their inmost hearts, as adjuncts and ornaments rather than as essential characteristics of a Christian life, and at all events never set it before themselves, as a test of the genuineness of their pro-

[1] Matt v 15, Mark iv 21, Luke viii. 16; ch xi. 33.

fession, that they be doing something for the perverse and crooked generation which surrounds them. If a man is once brought by God's grace to feel the responsibility of his lamp, the account which must be rendered hereafter for the trust committed to him, as respects others, in the possession by himself of the word of life, the second step will be far easier: the question how he is to hold it forth will almost answer itself in the asking: he has only to think what are those channels of influence through which he is capable of acting; he has only to ask what, under God, would be most impressive and most persuasive to himself, in the way of influence, if he were still in the gall of bitterness and in the bond of iniquity[1]; and then he will infer with certainty what he ought to attempt and how best he may succeed with others, how he may hope, always in dependence upon his Master's help, upon his Saviour's blessing, so to present and apply the light of his Gospel, that it shall shine into some now darkened heart and be reflected from some now crooked and perverse life.

2. I will mention two and but two of these modes of influence: and the former of these must plainly be example. *That they, seeing your good works*, our Saviour said, *may glorify your Father which is in heaven.*

i It would be quite idle to enlarge for the ten thousandth time upon the force of example. I may

[1] Acts viii 23.

assume that there is no engine, on the whole, so powerful in its effects upon human life. When you would present to another the word of life, you must do so, first of all, by example. Let him see how you live. Let him see that you do what Christ has commanded, that you turn away from that which Christ has forbidden, even when, in the one case, it is difficult, even when, in the other case, it is most attractive. No one can set limits to the operation of a consistent example. Men are never too old, and certainly they are never too young, to be struck by it. Who could not tell the names of one or two godly men in this town, whose influence is felt where it is least acknowledged? men whose life, however quiet, however unobtrusive, is known to be spent in the endeavour to do good, to promote in every possible way the glory of God and the welfare of His creatures? In such cases we see what may be called the standing witness of an exemplary life. These men are the proof to us that there is such a thing as vital godliness; that there is such a thing as living for another world[1] and counting all things else but loss[2] in comparison with it. In the most neglected place, in a village where within human memory there has not been heard the sound of a pure and genuine Gospel, you will find one or two lives of this sort testifying to the power of the grace of God to work without means or against means as effectually as with

[1] Heb. xi. 14. [2] Phil. iii. 8.

means and by means. You can scarcely account for these cases but on the supposition that Christ lives and reigns, and that the God of nature and of Providence is also the God of grace. He never leaves Himself wholly without witness[1], nor the creatures of His hand without examples of the working of His Spirit.

And that which is true of the general effect of a holy and Christian life is true also of its particular results. A young man—I cite a familiar instance— happens on a journey to share the same room with a casual companion. The one goes to his bed prayerless: the other kneels down to commune with his God and Saviour before he commits himself to rest. The consequence is, under God's controlling hand, observation, enquiry, reflection; at last, a converted heart; at last, a saved soul. That was an instance—I doubt not there have been a thousand such instances—of a Christian man *holding forth the word of life* by a particular act harmonizing with the constant tenor of a holy example. Whose heart has not been made ashamed, sorry sometimes with a godly sorrow[2], by the sight of some humbler or busier man, perhaps of some tender and delicate woman[3], going forth, regardless of health or weather, to perform some regular and unostentatious act of piety or charity, from which the observer has hitherto, it may be, stood aloof? Has not the effect of example, in such an instance, sometimes

[1] Acts xiv. 17.   [2] 2 Cor. vii. 9, 10.   [3] Deut. xxviii. 56.

been this—self-reproach, exertion, imitation; at last perhaps, for in these things the beginning is half the whole, a life redeemed altogether from indolence and self-indulgence to the active service of a God and Saviour?

11   But there is a second and a scarcely less powerful engine, for that application, of which the text speaks, of the word of life: and that is sympathy. There is a way of presenting the Gospel, in word, and even in example, which wholly fails to attract or to persuade. There is a dry, cold, harsh, stern mode of expressing the truth: and there is a repulsive, ungenial, precise, stiff sort of example which never leads men, seeing its good works, to glorify a Father who is in heaven. It becomes one who would discharge his conscience in this matter to examine not only the correctness but the attractiveness of his example. To the young more especially, but not to the young only, it is of the first importance that religion should be made, as it essentially is, a beautiful and a winning thing. *He that winneth souls is wise*[1]*:* not, he that alarms, or he that drives, or he that coerces and constrains, but *he that winneth souls.* Let a man, let a child, see that you feel for him and feel with him, feel for his poverty, or feel for his sorrow, or feel for his restless, unsatisfied, starved and friendless soul; feel for it, not as a superior being might feel, free himself

[1] Prov. xi 30.

from the like experience or the like possibility, but as one who is himself also compassed with infirmity[1], just as sinful by nature, just as desolate, just as unhappy without Christ, but having found rest and peace in believing, and now desirous, out of love, to draw others into the same region of peace and light; let this be so —and if it be, there will be no distance of manner, no studied condescension, no harshness of rebuke, and no formality of statement, but a free, open, generous heartiness, and a warm, ungrudging, compassionate sympathy—let all this, I say, be so—and depend upon it, you will gain access by degrees into the citadel of that man's soul; not all at once, not without long patience, not without an indefatigable importunity; but at last it will yield, in your Master's name you will enter in, and a charity which was Christian indeed will have won a victory which the purest of examples without it would have failed to achieve

3 I will end with a few words of practical counsel.

Much is lost, in spiritual as in worldly things, by too vague and discursive an aim. As long as we think generally of shining as lights in the world, though it is well that we should desire to do so, and the idea is Scriptural and therefore true, there will be something of unreality in the conception: beyond being careful to give no offence[2], no cause of stumbling, to any one, and to maintain an unreproving conscience in the

[1] Heb. v 2.   [2] 2 Cor. vi. 3.

sight of God and men[1], we shall have no definite goal in view, we shall be running uncertainly[2], and therefore not attaining. Let us make the matter more practical by greatly narrowing its bounds. Let us review our position, beginning with home itself. Is all right there? Is every member of your family the object of your direct care and concern in a spiritual sense? I hope you are not extinguishing your lamp at home, that you may keep it entirely for out-door use. I hope you are careful to *hold forth*, that is, to apply, *the word of life* to your own household first of all, and to each one amongst them as opportunity is given. If then you are the master or head of a household, you will be mindful of the duty of family prayer, as one, and the most direct, means of presenting the light of life to those for whom you are responsible. And you will pray for them all, as well as with them. There is no such thing as making the light shine by a mere human attention to its supply and to its trimming. God must be called in: and this, I would repeat, not vaguely for all, but personally too for each. Remember, those within your own doors see you as none else can. If there is any weak point in your example, any defect in your armour, anything wrong in temper, in speech, in habit or conduct, it is seen there, by wife and children, by servants and dependents, as it may not be seen perhaps by acquaintances or strangers. And this

[1] Acts xxiv. 16. [2] 1 Cor. ix. 26.

defect, whatever it be, goes much against your holding forth the word of life   They must respect before they will listen. Here therefore is an added reason for watchfulness. If you would truly discharge the Christian duty of presenting your lamp of life to be the guide of their steps, you must see to it that it first guide your own.

But never can a minister of Christ in this town counsel any one who cares for the Gospel to confine his labours in its behalf to his own home-circle   Let each one have a few poor persons, if it be but ten or but five houses in some one of our yards or lanes, into which he steadily sets himself to carry the light of life. We want a large subdivision of labour to effect anything. What is one visit in a month to a house every inmate of which needs the voice of Christian instruction and the hand of Christian sympathy? We want a hundred visitors, men and women, to do that work which must wait till the Spirit of God breathes upon the souls of His servants an apostolical zeal and a Christ-like self-devotion. Then will something be done. Then, and then only. *Upon the land of my people shall come up thorns and briars; yea, upon all the houses of joy in the joyous city...until the Spirit be poured upon us from on high, and the wilderness be a fruitful field, and the fruitful field be counted for a forest.   Then judgment shall dwell in the wilderness, and righteousness remain in the fruitful field.   And the work of righteousness shall be peace; and the effect of righteousness quietness and assurance for ever......Blessed are ye that sow beside all waters, that send forth thither the feet of the ox and the ass*[1]. God grant that that day may come surely, come speedily—and that our eyes may see it!

[1] Isai. xxxii. 13—20

SECOND SUNDAY AFTER CHRISTMAS,
January 5, 1862

LECTURE X.

PHILIPPIANS II. 17—24.

17 *Nay, if I am even poured as a drink-offering upon the sacrifice and ministration of your faith, I rejoice, and rejoice*
18 *with you all. And in the same respect do ye also rejoice, and rejoice with me.*

19 *And I hope in the Lord Jesus speedily to send you Timotheus, that I also may be of good heart when I have learned*
20 *the things which concern you. For I have no one likeminded— one who will sincerely be anxious about the things which*
21 *concern you. For they all seek their own things, not the*
22 *things of Christ Jesus. But the test of him ye know, that as a child with a father he served with me unto the Gospel.*
23 *Him therefore I hope to send, so soon as I shall have clearly*
24 *seen the things which concern me, forthwith, and I trust, in the Lord, that I myself also shall speedily come*

LECTURE X.

PHILIPPIANS II. 20

I have no man likeminded.

IN some of St Paul's writings the Apostle predominates, in others the man. In the Epistles to the Romans, for example, and to the Ephesians, we have large disclosures of Christian truth and Christian doctrine · we have but little comparatively of personal allusion or personal appeal. In both these cases there is a reason for this. The Epistle to the Romans was written to a congregation which he had neither formed nor as yet visited. The Epistle to the Ephesians was probably a circular letter; designed for transmission to other Churches besides that to which he had, for three years at one time, personally ministered. Where he writes, as he writes here, to a congregation first gathered by himself, well known by face and character, and presenting marked features of excellence or else of defect, every word is stamped with the impress of a living man, full of feeling, full of energy, full of fire, and the interest of the communication is largely increased by the very circumstance which distinguishes it altogether from an essay, from a sermon, or from an oration.

The passage upon which we enter, but which we shall scarcely conclude, this morning—extending from the 17th verse to the close of the second chapter—has suggested this remark. We feel throughout it that we are dealing with a man; a man of like passions and like affections with ourselves; yet also a man who lived a life far above ours, and had a firm hold upon those invisible realities which are often to us so shadowy and so remote.

He has said, in a verse already considered, that he would have those whom he addresses to *shine as lights in the world, holding forth,* applying, or presenting, for the guidance and comfort of others, that *word of life*[1] which has first been received and felt within. And for this amongst other reasons, that he *may rejoice (triumph) in the day of Christ,* in the consciousness, confirmed by their safety and glory, *that he ran not* on earth *in vain, nor laboured in vain.* He then enlarges upon this thought, this twofold thought, of his devotion to them, and of his joy in its success.

Nay, if I am even offered, or more exactly, *if I am even poured as a drink-offering, upon the sacrifice and*

[1] *Verse* 16.

ministration of your faith, I rejoice, and rejoice with you all[1]. The Levitical Law contained directions that, with the daily morning and evening sacrifice of a lamb upon God's altar, there should always be offered a meat-offering of flour mingled with oil, and a drink-offering of a specified quantity of wine[2]. The expression before us is borrowed from that ordinance. *If I am even poured as a drink-offering upon the sacrifice and ministration of your faith.* Notice the terms. There is a sacrifice being offered; *your faith.* The genuine, living, working faith of Christian men and Christian women is that daily sacrifice, *holy, acceptable to God*[3], which the Epistle for last Sunday bade us all continually to present. It is not indeed a sacrifice of propitiation. Nothing that we can do in the service of God or man could ever take away sin. Nor is that needful. Christ has done that, once for all, by His one oblation of Himself once offered[4]. Ours is a sacrifice offered on the strength of His. Not to add to it, not to complete it, as though it lacked anything; but on the strength of it, as that which has alone made any human offering acceptable, as that in virtue of which every human being may bring his offering with confidence. *By Him let us offer the sacrifice of praise to God continually*[5]. *To whom coming...ye also...are built up a spiritual house, an*

---

[1] *Verse* 17. [2] Exod. xxix. 38, &c.; Numb. xxviii. 3, &c.
[3] Rom. xii. 1. [4] Heb. x. 10, 14. [5] Heb. xiii. 15.

holy priesthood, to offer up spiritual sacrifices, acceptable to God by Jesus Christ[1].

Now this sacrifice, of a living faith, of a faithful life, is here spoken of as offered by the help of a human minister. St Peter, in a passage just referred to, describes Christians as offering their own spiritual sacrifices. St Paul, by a slight variation of the same figure, describes himself as offering the sacrifice of others. Thus in another Epistle he speaks of *the grace given him of God, that he should be the minister of Jesus Christ to the Gentiles, ministering the Gospel of God, that the offering up of the Gentiles* by him *might be acceptable, being sanctified by the Holy Ghost*[2]. And thus here *The sacrifice and service of your faith*. The faith of the Philippian Christians is a sacrifice in which he assists, at which he ministers. As Christ Himself is the heavenly Priest, whose mediation alone makes the sacrifice availing, so the Apostle of Christ is the earthly priest, by whose hands it has pleased God that the sacrifice should be ministered. *The sacrifice and ministration of your faith.*

And he goes one step further. With this sacrifice of the Christian life, in which he is engaged as the officiating priest below, there must be a drink-offering presented upon God's altar. And that drink-offering is the life-blood of the officiating priest Himself. St Paul's own blood is to be poured as it were upon the

---

[1] 1 Pet. ii. 4, &c. [2] Rom. xv. 15, 16.

sacrifice of their faith. If it be so, he says, if even to that extent his devotion to Christ and Christ's people must be carried, to the extent of martyrdom itself in their service, he will still rejoice in himself, and rejoice with them.

And in the same respect, in the same way, *do ye also rejoice, and rejoice with me*[1]. Rejoice in the thought of those blessings into which my ministry has admitted you; and forget not me in your joy; *rejoice, and rejoice with me*.

And I hope, in the Lord Jesus, in whom, as a member of whom, by whose suggestion and in dependence upon whose blessing, all my plans are laid, and without whom nothing is undertaken, *speedily to send you Timotheus, that I also may be of good heart when I have learned the things which concern you*[2]. You see what real Christian anxiety is; a genuine disinterested concern for the welfare in soul and body of those who are loved and cared for. *For I have no one else likeminded* with myself *who will sincerely (genuinely) be anxious about the things which concern you*[3]*: for they all seek their own things*, the things which belong to themselves, their own interests, their own comfort and welfare, *not the things of Christ Jesus*[4]. *But the test of him ye know*, the test which has been applied to him and under which he has not failed, namely, *that as a child with a father he served*

[1] *Verse* 18. [2] *Verse* 19. [3] *Verse* 20. [4] *Verse* 21.

with me unto, in furtherance of, *the Gospel*[1]. You yourselves saw, in my visits to you in company with Timotheus, how dutifully and how tenderly he shared my toils in the service of the Gospel of Christ. *Him therefore I hope to send, as soon as I shall have clearly seen the things which concern me,* the result of my imprisonment, *forthwith*[2]*: and I trust, in the Lord,* in dependence upon Christ, *that I myself also shall speedily come*[3]. He has expressed in the first chapter a somewhat confident expectation that his present danger will not be unto death[4]; that he shall not die, but live[5], and labour on yet longer for the good of all the Churches. And here he says that one of his first acts, after his release (if it be so) from imprisonment, will be a journey to Philippi.

From the eight verses thus briefly opened, the topic selected for especial notice this morning is, the experience of isolation. *I have no man likeminded.*

It is a common complaint amongst us, that we want sympathy. We are lonely, we say. If not actually solitary, we are solitary in feeling and in heart. How many do I address this morning, whose secret cry, as it enters into the ear of a compassionate Lord above, is this and this chiefly, *I have no one likeminded!* In later life people make up their minds to this, as a condition of earthly life. They have fought

---

[1] *Verse* 22.   [2] *Verse* 23.   [3] *Verse* 24.
[4] Phil. i. 25.   [5] Psalm cxviii. 17.

against it in youth. They have deemed it intolerable. They have thought existence itself valueless without sympathy. Now and then they have fancied for a brief time that they had found a sympathy real and indestructible below. But they have outlived the hope. They have known perhaps many such hopes, one by one, and they have outlived them all. It is well if they have not too much acquiesced in this experience. It is well if they have not become, by age and by disappointment, too entirely isolated and self-contained. That is one of the dangers of age, as the other is a danger of youth. The young are too impatient, too imperious, in their demand for sympathy: the old are sometimes too tolerant, at last too fond, of isolation.

And there is much that is fanciful, much that is morbid, in that complaint of the young, that they have no one likeminded. It is often heard from the heart of a quiet and a Christian home, where brothers and sisters are living together in what, but for themselves, might be almost a paradise of contentment. Why cannot that sister find her sympathy within her own doors? Why cannot she make one of her own household the repository of her troubles and the sharer of her joys? No, that is too tame and too commonplace a friendship · nothing but that which is spontaneous, self-made and self-sought, has any charms for one who is as yet trying new sources of happiness instead of drinking thankfully of those which God has opened. And sometimes this search, this irritating, enfeebling, fruitless search, goes on through a great part of human life. The time never comes when the mistake is rightly seen and frankly confessed. Far beyond the days of imagination and romance the search is still protracted, after that undefined and indefinable kind or degree of sympathy, which shall make earth at last a fairyland, and restore us, not through grace but through nature, to the Eden which sin once forfeited.

The words of St Paul give no encouragement to this ungrateful, this thankless pursuit. St Paul says indeed, and in the tone of complaint, *I have no man likeminded*. He was a man of quick and deep feeling, of warm affections and of great aspirations. We cannot read a line of his Epistles without perceiving that he was a man to whom life without love would have been a constant torture, a daily death. Whatever he may have been in the days of his ignorance, while he was persecuting Christianity[1] as a crime and looking on complacently upon the cruel death of martyrs[2]— and even then, no doubt, he knew what it was to love warmly within the narrower circle to which, as a matter of duty, he confined his sympathies—yet at all events when he became a Christian, he entered with his whole soul into the world-wide charities of the

[1] Acts viii. 1.   [2] Acts ix. 1.

Gospel, and found in the permission, in the command, to love all men and to lay down life itself for human happiness, not only the strongest of attractions towards the faith of Christ, but the most convincing proof also that that faith itself was of Divine origin.

Nor was his a promiscuous love only. Within the universal brotherhood he had also his special preferences and his close attachments. There were congregations, like that of Philippi, which he loved with a more than common ardour. There were fellow-helpers, fellow-soldiers, companions in toil and in tribulation, brothers and sons too in the Gospel, who were more to him than other men, than even other Christian men, were to him; in whose society he found a peculiar joy, in whose departure, pain, or death he sorrowed with a peculiar grief. In all these things St Paul was entirely one of ourselves He knew what it was to crave for sympathy; and he knew what it was to pine in isolation. Even amongst Christian duties, even in Christian society, he sometimes felt his heart lonely, because a particular friend was absent[1], or because a particular congregation was in circumstances of distress or peril[2]. His character was as human as it was Christian

But it is needful to correct this impression by another. St Paul's thirst for human love was not that sentimental, sickly, vague, purposeless thing which

[1] 2 Cor. ii. 12, 13.   [2] 1 Thess. ii 17, ch iii 1

may sometimes amongst us take its name. It was not with him, as it too often is with us, that his heart's best affections were roving in quest of an object, and that, until that object presented itself in some human form, he was a restless and dissatisfied man. St Paul's best affections were engaged and fixed unalterably. *To me,* he said, *to live is Christ*[1] *No longer I, but Christ liveth in me*[2]. His life was *hid with Christ in God*[3]. What he sought in human friendship was not a supreme, nor even a subordinate object of affection When he was lonely and comfortless in the lack of human sympathy, it was not because he missed something on which self might rest and from which self might draw either support or soothing No, it was with him, as the text tells us, a widely different thing from any of these. The sympathy he sought was a sympathy in his work for Christ: the loneliness he bewailed was a loneliness in his care for Christ's people. *I have no man likeminded, who will naturally care for your state: for all seek their own, not the things which are Jesus Christ's.* How noble, how unselfish, a complaint! What a lesson does it suggest to us who are here assembled to-day! How it breathes altogether a spirit of Christian devotion, of divine compassion! How it rises above lower regards and meaner motives, and shews a heart engrossed in the service of a heavenly Master, in the

[1] Phil 1. 21   [2] Gal ii 20.   [3] Col iii 3.

endeavour to finish faithfully and to finish successfully a work given him from above! How it says to us, Away with your little, selfish, earth-born murmurings! What means this cherishing of lonely feelings, this complaint of having no one to share with you your trials, doubts, and flittings? So long as your troubles are all selfish, they cannot be borne too lonelily So long as all your concern is about natural frames and feelings, about things in which God is not, in which Christ is not, so long you cannot expect to taste of Christian love, the comfort of a Christian sympathy. In these things those who will suffer must suffer. Change your ground altogether. Come first to Christ: give yourself first to Him: accept His salvation with the heart: undertake His service with your life dash away these encumbering fetters of self and sin, and rise into that region where God is, where Christ sitteth at the right hand of God: and then, when this is done, then begin to ask for some one likeminded, some one with whom you may exchange thoughts and feelings elevating then and not enfeebling, profitable then and not (as now) worthless, some one who may work with you, some one who may hope with you, some one who may learn with you, some one who may improve and advance with you, some one who may at length, when life's fitful fever is ended, even rest with you and rise with you —for thus and thus only can you know either true sympathy or true friendship, when it springs out of the common love of Christ, and when it is exercised in common work for Christ. This was the friendship for which St Paul thirsted: this was that sympathy for which he could accept no counterfeit, and in the absence of which he counted himself isolated and desolate.

And if sympathy like this be still, as it sometimes was to St Paul, denied or interrupted, yet even then we shall learn, like him, *in whatever state we are, therewith to be content*[1]. If we indeed possess the love of Christ, we must not be impatient for any other. If we really love Christ, and are trying day by day to serve Him, we have within us the root of all comfort, and the spring of all sympathy. They who are united in Him are united really in each other. They may see it, or not see it: they may be conscious of human communion, or unconscious: but they who are one in Christ are one also with each other. And therefore, whatever befalls you, you may take comfort in the thought that you are not indeed alone in it. Others are sharing with you in that experience. Are you in poverty? are you in distress? are you suffering from bereavement? are you mourning in the sense of sin? do you spend many a lonely hour? is your home stripped of its treasures, and your heart of those with whom it once took sweetest counsel? Yet remember, you have with you, unseen but not unfelt, the com-

[1] Phil iv 11.

munion of saints, the converse, through Him your Head, of all the redeemed whether in earth or heaven; their prayers are with you, and their sympathies are with you; they have been before you, or else they are beside you, in your journey, and they will welcome or else follow you into the everlasting habitations[1]. That sympathy, which to the worldly man and the sinner is impossible (in its highest sense) with any, is yours with all.

And O above all this, far, far above, yours is the sympathy of Christ Himself. He—let it be said with reverence—is Himself likeminded with you; interested in your state, concerned in your work, desirous of your welfare, yea, pledged and bound by the ties of an eternal love to your victory and your salvation. If He be with you, who can be against you[2]? If He be with you, where can loneliness be, or desolation, or desertion? Yet a little while, and all shall be bright with you, all peaceful, all glorious. Never will you accuse, from the other side of the dark valley and of the cold stream, that sense of isolation which drove you nearer to your Saviour, that want of earthly sympathy which made you cling more resolutely to the heavenly. There take refuge. there find rest and He Himself, even Jesus Christ, your Lord and your God, will repair every breach, comfort every sorrow,

[1] Luke xvi. 9.   [2] Rom. viii. 31, &c.

wipe away all tears from your face, and at last, as it is written, *swallow up death* itself *in victory*[1].

[1] Isai. xxv. 8.

SECOND SUNDAY AFTER THE EPIPHANY,
January 19, 1862.

LECTURE XI.

PHILIPPIANS II. 25—30.

25   *But I thought it necessary to send to you Epaphroditus,
my brother and fellow-workman and fellow-soldier, and your
26 messenger and minister to my need, for he was longing after
you all, and in great trouble, because ye heard that he was
27 sick.   For indeed he was sick, close upon death   but God had
pity on him, and not on him only, but on me also, lest I should
28 have sorrow upon sorrow.   I send him therefore the more
eagerly, that seeing him ye may again be glad, and I may be
29 less sorrowful.   Receive him therefore in the Lord with all
30 joy, and hold such men in honour, because for the work's
sake he drew nigh even unto death, having hazarded*[1] *his life
that he might fill up your deficiency in the ministration
towards me.*

[1] Literally, *having counselled ill for his life*, or according to another reading, *having been venturesome with his life*.

LECTURE XI[1].

PHILIPPIANS II. 27.

He was sick, nigh unto death: but God had mercy on him.

I TRUST in the Lord Jesus, St Paul has said above, *to send Timotheus shortly to you*[2]...*I trust in the Lord that I also myself shall come shortly*[3]. Yet, notwithstanding this hope, this twofold hope, he defers not longer the return of their own messenger, but sends him back to Philippi with these words of tender and loving counsel. Such is the general substance of the half paragraph on which we now enter. We shall find it, I am persuaded, full of arguments for that work of Christian charity to which I am to invite you to-day.

But I thought it necessary to send to you Epaphro-

[1] A Collection was made on this occasion for the District Visiting Society of the Parish.

[2] *Verse* 19   [3] *Verse* 24.

ditus, my brother and fellow-workman and fellow-soldier, and your messenger and minister to my need[1]. Of Epaphroditus we know nothing but what this Epistle tells. The fourth chapter expressly states, what is here plainly indicated, that he had been employed by the Philippian Church to carry a contribution to St Paul's wants during his long imprisonment at Rome[2]. He describes him very beautifully as not only his kind benefactor on the part of the Philippians on this occasion, but as also his brother, and his companion in all the toils and in all the conflicts of the Christian life below.

He has resolved to send him back without further loss of time. *For he was longing after you all, and in great trouble*[3]. It is the same word which describes our Lord's condition at the beginning of His agony: *He began to be sorrowful and* very heavy[4]...*began to be sore amazed and to be* very heavy[5]. *In great trouble, because ye heard that he was sick.* He knows that the tidings of his illness have reached you, and he knows how much you will be distressed. This makes him impatient to return and to reassure you. The report you have heard is too true *For indeed he was sick, close upon death: but God had pity on him, and not on him only, but on me also, lest I should have sorrow upon sorrow*[6], lest the sorrow of losing him should be

---

[1] *Verse* 25. [2] Phil. iv. 18. [3] *Verse* 26.
[4] Matt. xxvi. 37. [5] Mark xiv. 33. [6] *Verse* 27.

added to the sorrow of imprisonment and loneliness.

I send him therefore the more eagerly, with more readiness and despatch than I should otherwise have used, *that seeing him ye may again be glad, and I may be less sorrowful*[1]. The thought of your joy in seeing him again will be a comfort to me, it will lighten my sorrow.

Receive him therefore in the Lord[2]—not as a mere human friend, but in the exercise of a higher union in Christ your Lord—*with all joy; and hold such men in honour; because for the work's sake,* out of love to the cause of that Gospel for which I am suffering, *he drew nigh even unto death, having hazarded his life, that he might fill up your deficiency in the ministration towards me*[3], that he might perform that part of the work of ministering to my need, which you, from absence and distance, could not do, that he might represent you in that personal service towards me from which circumstances debarred you

Of the cause and nature of the sickness mentioned in the text we know nothing. Whether a hasty journey, whether the discomforts of his sojourn in Rome, whether the closeness of his attendance upon the imprisoned Apostle, whether any or all of these things may have been the cause of the malady, we know not We know only that it was a sickness

[1] *Verse* 28.   [2] *Verse* 29.   [3] *Verse* 30.

nearly fatal, and that it was incurred in the service of St Paul, and thus *for the work of Christ.*

1. *He was sick.* The thought of sickness is suggested to us naturally by the appeal made to you to-day. It is to sickness most of all, though not exclusively, that the charitable ministry now to be provided for is directed. And it is a salutary thing for the healthy and the active to remember those who are in sickness. What a change does sickness, even of a slight kind, make in our thoughts and feelings! What a real, and what a powerful thing, is the hand then laid upon us! What an importance does it give to things at other times trivial, and what an insignificance to things at other times engrossing! The strong man is then in the grasp of a stronger. The worldly man finds then that there is something as true as the things that are seen. The busy man is reminded that there will be an end of work, and the frivolous man that there will be an end of pleasure

And what a natural incongruity is there between health and sickness—yes, between the sick and the healthy! How does the very presence of a person in robust health jar upon the sensitiveness of a frame diseased! How few are there whose visit to a chamber of sickness carries with it repose and soothing! Quick movements, loud tones, and promiscuous topics, how do they all interfere with the proprieties, with the sanctities, of a sick room! We do not always think enough of these things—we whose office carries us into scenes of suffering. We do not always remember as we ought the probabilities and the possibilities of a condition of disease. What a tenderness should we cherish towards the peculiarities, towards the frailties, yes, towards the fancies and the irritabilities, of sickness! What care should be shewn in the choice of times, in the control of speech and motion, still more in the selection of topics and in the regard to brevity! And yet, again, in all these things, how should art conceal art! let me rather say, how should a delicate consideration prompt everything, and a natural refinement guide without effort to the right and suitable thing! How should we study without studying, guard without guarding, and consider without premeditating!

God gives these gifts naturally to some: and some others acquire them in the school of Jesus Depend upon it, they are matters of first importance to all who, whether as Clergymen or as District Visitors, would do the work of ministers to suffering. What can we expect to result from their visitation, who in a spirit of self-satisfaction, with a tone of superiority and a manner of rigidity, enter that door on which poverty or distress has set its seal, or pass to that chamber in which a wasting and pining sickness has relaxed every energy and wellnigh cut off communication with the living? O for the spirit of that divine charity which *suffereth long and is kind*, which *vaunteth not itself, is not puffed up, is not provoked, and thinketh no evil*[1]*!* that charity which throws its soul into the circumstances of the suffering, and actually weeps with them that weep[2]! that charity without which a man might even bestow all his goods to feed the poor[3], and yet be nothing, and yet receive nothing from the Lord[4]!

2. *He was sick, nigh unto death* There is power, we have seen, even in a slight sickness, to change the thoughts of health, and to fix a wide gulf between the strong and the diseased. There is profit too, for those who are taught of God, in the temporary suspension thus occasioned of the occupations and the feelings of robust health. Happy are they who well use—for indeed such use comes not necessarily nor easily—those seasons of passing indisposition which interrupt from time to time a life of average vigour! They will find themselves the less surprised and the less overwhelmed by the arrival of that time which must come at last to all of us, when a sickness not slight but mortal shall *darken the windows* for ever and *loose*, as it is written, *the silver cord of life*[5].

But there are those, I doubt not, in this congregation, who have known something more than slight interruptions, temporary suspensions, of the great gift

[1] 1 Cor xiii 4, 5.   [2] Rom. xii 15.   [3] 1 Cor xiii 3
[4] James i. 7.   [5] Eccles. xii. 3, 6.

of health *He was sick*, St Paul writes of his friend, *close upon death*. And he says again, *he drew nigh even unto death*. This is an experience more notable than rare. This sort of visit to the gates of the grave, this acquaintance with the preliminaries, though not with the act itself, of dying, this near approach to the invisible world, yet without entering it for ever, is an occurrence by no means infrequent in the way of accident or of disease We are all familiar with records of one particular class of human disaster, perils by river and perils by sea, in which every stage of the process of dying has been travelled through, down to that state of unconsciousness in which the bitterness of death itself is past. How remarkable— it may truly be said, how fearful—are the details of these records! Words and acts long forgotten— deeds done in youth, nay, in early childhood—omissions of duty so far gone by that for years they have neither been felt as guilt nor remembered in confession—little trifles of boyish violence or of childish disobedience and selfishness—have flashed again upon the mind, in those few moments of drowning, with the quickness of intuition and in all the combination and coherence of a picture. and they have made a person able, when he came back to the living, to tell from experience how it may be with all men in the judgment, how without witnesses and without an accuser, without any processes of investigation or any formalities of adjudication, conscience itself may arraign the sinner at the bar of God, and conscience itself be charged with the final office of the executioner and the tormentor, of the undying worm and the unquenched fire[1]

But sickness too, as well as accident, may give something of the same experience. There may have been a long suspense between life and death. The sentence of the physician may have destroyed hope, and the battle between the unaided forces of nature and the strength of the last enemy may have been waged for hours in the sight of agonized friends powerless to succour or to alleviate. At last a turn has come: the sickness was *close upon death*, but it was not death itself: and all this agony, all this mortal strife, must be endured again hereafter. The soul has come back from the gates of the grave by a process almost of resurrection. The life of earth must begin again, with all its trials, uncertainties, and contradictions. Has that person, think you, nothing to tell of those days of expected dissolution? Can that person ever again lose the experience there acquired? Was there not a peculiarity, a singularity, a uniqueness, in that view of death so near, so instant? We know indeed that nothing, not even such an experience, can of itself convert a soul, or ensure a life of faith and of holiness in the days thus marvel-

[1] Isai. lxvi 24; Mark ix 44

lously prolonged. *If they hear not Moses and the prophets, neither will they be persuaded though one rose from the dead*[1]—*neither will they be persuaded*, thus might we supplement the words of inspiration, *though they themselves came back again from the dead.* But at least they will tell how small and how poor the world looked, from within the curtains of that seeming deathbed; how true God's truth appeared then, how holy His holiness, how important His salvation, how formidable His judgment; how time and eternity had then interchanged, without an effort, their relative value, and nothing seemed worthy of a care or an endeavour, which was not of God and which was not for ever. O if I address any such to-day, any who have once been sick nigh unto death, but who are now again in health and strength among the living, well may I ask of them whether indeed they have duly cherished the impression made upon them in those days of suspense, whether they have carefully kept, by God's help, the resolution with which they rose again from the bed of suffering, *I will walk before the Lord in the land of the living*[2].

3. *He was sick, nigh unto death: but God had mercy on him.*

Is this the same Apostle, who wrote above, *I have a desire to depart, and to be with Christ; which is far better*[3]? Does he account it a mercy on the part

[1] Luke xvi. 31.   [2] Psalm cxvi. 9.   [3] Phil. i. 23.

of God which withdraws a Christian man from the immediate fruition of the inheritance of the saints in light[1]? The words are so: and lest we should too much qualify their meaning, or say that the mercy spoken of was shewn not to the man himself, but to those around him, who needed his ministration or might be benefited by his life, he adds immediately afterwards, *And not on him only, but on me also, lest I should have sorrow upon sorrow.*

He was sick nigh unto death, but God had mercy on him, and brought him back for a while into the life which he had seemed to be quitting

We may gather from this saying an illustration of the naturalness of the Word of God. However bright the light which the Gospel throws upon the world beyond death, and however dim by comparison the glory which shines upon the present, still life is a blessing . *truly the light is sweet, and a pleasant thing it is for the eyes to behold the sun*[2]. And still death is an enemy, and the sentence, *Dust thou art, and unto dust shalt thou return*[3], a curse in itself, though it be relieved and transformed by the hopes and promises of the Gospel. To speak of death itself as a pleasure is a fantastic and unreal language. To speak of a recovery from sickness as a misfortune is as contradictory to the language of the Bible as it is to the voice of nature within. Who does not feel that a

[1] Col 1 12.   [2] Eccl. xi. 7.   [3] Gen. iii 19.

restoration from what had seemed like a fatal sickness is a reason, as our own Church teaches us, for giving *humble and hearty thanks to* that God who is *the Lord of life and death, and of all things to them pertaining*[1]?

No one, I suppose, would doubt this in the case of one whose salvation is as yet less than secure. For an unforgiven and impenitent sinner to be brought back from death must be a gift of God's mercy in the thought of all men. That a man has not been cut off in his sins, that a new opportunity is given him for repentance and amendment of life, that he has time still allowed him, even when it seemed almost hopeless, to break off his sins by righteousness[2], that he has a new mark of God's goodness impressed upon him, and a new motive, if he be not utterly hardened, for faith and calling upon God, this surely must be a cause for thankfulness: well may we say of such a man, *He was sick, nigh unto death; but God had mercy on him*

But Epaphroditus was a Christian man. He was spoken of by St Paul as a brother, a fellow-workman, and a fellow-soldier. He had incurred his sickness by faith and love, not regarding his life, for the work of Christ To him, if to any man, death would have been gain. And doubtless, if God's Providence had so

---

[1] General Thanksgiving Visitation of the Sick.
[2] Dan. iv. 27.

ordered it, St Paul would have bidden his Philippian friends to give thanks over him as over one who safely slept in Jesus. He would have taught them not to sorrow for him[1], but to rejoice with a joy unspeakable and full of glory[2].

Yes, my brethren, it is even so The word of the Gospel has ever two aspects. If God wills this, it is well for the Christian. And if God wills the opposite of this, yet for the Christian it is well still. If he lives, that is the fruit of his labour[3]: he can still work on, gather in more souls for Christ, shine more brightly himself as he holds forth the word of life. If he rises from this bed of sickness, he rises a better man; more humble, more watchful, more devoted; more bent upon using every power of his body, and every faculty of his mind, for the honour of Him to whom he owes all things. If he has still to wage a little longer his anxious warfare, surely it is because there was need of him below; because there was something in him still to be improved, because there was something by him still to be done. Therefore, if his heavy sickness is not unto death, we say, as he returns from his chamber into the busy haunts of life, *God had mercy on him*.

And if he rises not, if he lives not, if he passes only from his bed to his coffin, from his chamber to his grave, even then, then even more, shall we say,

[1] 1 Thess. iv. 13.   [2] 1 Pet. i. 8.   [3] Phil 1 22.

God had mercy on him, saw that he was ready, and therefore took him; saw the field within white to the harvest, and therefore thrust in the sickle and reaped it[1]; saw that he was meet for the inheritance above, and therefore, by a transition sharp but blessed, bade him enter in, and rest for ever in the Lord. *This is the heritage of the servants of the Lord, and their righteousness is of me, saith the Lord*[2].

The time has arrived, at which you commonly enable your ministers to provide in some measure for the wants through a coming year of your poor and suffering neighbours. We have ever found you ready to respond to this call. It is one which you recognize as just and urgent. Many of those whom we here address, themselves aid us in the distribution. And thankful should we be if many more would come forward to aid personally in that good work. Nothing but a very minute subdivision can make the office of a District Visitor encouraging or satisfactory. From twenty to forty houses are as much as ought ever to fall to the charge of one person. We would gladly assign but ten houses, or five houses, to persons whose time or strength may be adequate to this charge and unequal to a heavier. We want, not inspectors, still less censors, but friends, of the poor. We want those who feel for distress as being themselves also compassed with infirmity. We want those

[1] Rev. xiv. 15   [2] Isai liv 17

who, like their Saviour Himself, can at once hate sin and love the sinner. God dispose many hearts amongst you, my beloved brethren, to undertake and even to covet this ministry! And may He give, to those who bear it, the zeal, and the wisdom, and the patience, and the sympathy, which are indispensable to its right discharge!

To the rest of the congregation, prevented, it may be, by other imperious calls of duty from assuming this office, yet not precluded by any calls of duty from giving yourselves in some form to the work of charity, we look, and not in vain, for those offerings of silver and gold which we may administer, in your behalf, to the sick and the poor of Christ's flock Thirty pounds, added to-day to the periodical offerings made through the year at the Lord's table, will furnish, if not all we need, yet all we ask of you. I know that we shall not ask in vain

THIRD SUNDAY AFTER THE EPIPHANY,
January 26, 1862.

LECTURE XII.

PHILIPPIANS III. 1—7.

1 FINALLY, my brethren, rejoice in the Lord To write the
same things to you, to me is not burdensome, and for you
2 is safe. Mark those who are dogs; mark the evil workmen,
2 mark the concision. For we are the circumcision, who by the
Spirit of God do service, and triumph in Christ Jesus, and
4 confide not in flesh, although I possess confidence even in flesh
5 If any other man thinks to confide in flesh, I more, in
circumcision one of the eighth day, of the race of Israel, of the
6 tribe of Benjamin, a Hebrew of Hebrews, in regard to law,
a Pharisee; in regard to zeal, a persecutor of the church, in
regard to righteousness, that (righteousness) which is in a law,
7 become blameless. But whatsoever things were to me gains,
these I have accounted for Christ's sake loss

LECTURE XII.

PHILIPPIANS III. 7.

What things were gain to me, those I counted loss for Christ.

FINALLY, *my brethren, rejoice in the Lord*[1]. So the chapter opens. And this word, joy, is, in fact, the keynote of the whole Epistle. The very last words, before the more personal topics introduced by the mention of Timotheus and Epaphroditus, were these: *I joy, and rejoice with you all.. For the same cause also do ye joy, and rejoice with me.* And even the more private topics which occupied the latter part of the second chapter are treated in reference to the same object, the comfort and joy of the writer and of those addressed If he purposes to send Timotheus to them, it is *that he may himself be of good comfort when he knows their state*[2]. If he sends back

[1] *Verse* 1.   [2] Phil. ii. 19

Epaphroditus to them with this letter, it is in the hope *that, when they see him again, they may rejoice, and that he himself,* in the reflection of their joy, *may be the less sorrowful*[1].

So natural, so harmonious, is the opening of the chapter now before us. *Finally, my brethren*—or *for the rest*—as for what remains to be said to you, it all amounts to this—*rejoice in the Lord.* See that you live in joy: and see that that joy be indeed a Christian joy; a joy springing out of, and constantly traceable to, your union with Christ by a true and living faith

I pause for a moment upon the words

Rejoice. It is a command It is not a wish, it is not a prayer, for them: it is a precept; it is an injunction; it is a command. Does any one here present think of joy as a duty? Are there none who almost cherish sorrow, dejection, depression, as a grace, or as a sign of grace? Let such person reflect upon the injunction here given. It will meet us again at a later point in the Epistle.

But the charge to rejoice stands not alone Not all joy is a duty. Joy may be worldly, may be frivolous, may be foolish, may be sinful *Rejoice in the Lord,* that is, in Christ, as persons who belong to Christ; who are something to Christ, and know it, who are concerned in what He has done, and in what He is,

---

[1] Chap ii 28

who are included in Christ, hidden in Christ, safe in Christ, for time and for eternity. Rejoice thus, and joy itself is not more a privilege than a duty.

To write the same things to you, to go on thus repeating the same thing to you, harping upon the same string,—joy, joy, joy—joy in tribulation, joy in sorrow, joy in the Lord—*to me is not burdensome*, I grudge not the trouble of it, *and for you is safe*, salutary and needful. You cannot be too often reminded of this great duty. It is only by frequent repetition that I can hope to impress upon you the urgency of its importance

But especially (it is as if he said) observe my words, *in the Lord* There are many who rejoice otherwise and on other grounds *Mark* carefully, and for avoidance, *those who are dogs*[1]; those who are in deed, what they are too ready to call others, *dogs* and not children. The inspired commentary upon the expression is found in that deeply affecting story of the Syrophœnician woman, for the trial of whose faith our Lord Himself used that very word which the proud Israelite was wont to apply to the less favoured Gentile, saying, *It is not meet to take the children's bread, and to cast it to dogs*[2]. St Paul here teaches the Church that those days of Jewish exclusiveness are for ever ended They to whom that appellation, so offensive to Jewish ears, is now

[1] *Verse* 2. [2] Matt. xv. 21—28.

appropriate, are not Gentiles but unbelievers; those who reject God's purpose of mercy in Christ Jesus, those, more especially, who either by their rapacity disgrace Christ's ministry, or by their unholiness defile Christ's body.

Mark the evil workmen[1]*;* those teachers who, professing (it may be) the faith of Christ, yet adulterate and nullify His salvation by mixing up the Law with it *mark* these men, and avoid them. We know how widely this leaven spread through the early churches St Paul's Epistles are full of warnings against it. St Paul's history is full of proofs of its influence. Even his beloved and faithful Philippians seem to have been in danger from it. Salvation by Christ must be a salvation all by Christ, or it is none.

Mark the concision. Observe, and avoid, those who tell you that, *except ye be circumcised after the manner of Moses, ye cannot be saved*[2] Such men call themselves *the circumcision*, the true Israelites, to whom alone God's promises are made but I call them rather *the concision, the mutilation:* so worthless becomes at once the ancient sign and sacrament of Judaism, when it has ceased, as it has now ceased, to be God's ordinance for His people.

For we are the circumcision[3], the true Israelite nation, who have a circumcision not outward but inward, *in the spirit and not in the letter*[4], even that

[1] 2 Cor. xi 13.   [2] Acts xv. 1.   [3] *Verse 3.*   [4] Rom ii 28, 29

putting off of the body of the sins of the flesh[1], of which the rite of circumcision was not the reality but the sign. *We are the* true *circumcision*, the true circumcised nation, *who by the Spirit of God do service*, who by the inward presence of the consecrating and transforming Spirit offer the sacrifice not of dead victims but of a devoted and renewed life[2], *and triumph*, make our boast, *in Christ Jesus*, not in ourselves, nor in anything that we have or do or are, *and confide not in flesh*, put no confidence in outward rites or carnal ordinances as securing to us the favour of God.

Though I, as well as others, *possess confidence*, that is, means and materials of confidence, if such there be, *even in flesh*[3]. The words are explained and guarded by what next follows *If any other man thinks to confide*, imagines himself to have materials for confidence, *in flesh*, in outward or carnal advantages, *I more;* still more might I do so, I who am *in circumcision one of the eighth day*[4]; not a proselyte, admitted into the Jewish covenant at a later point in life, but a born Israelite, circumcised on the prescribed and regular day; *of the race of Israel, of the tribe of Benjamin*, duly registered in one of the component tribes of Israel; *a Hebrew of Hebrews*, an Israelite by both parents: again, *in regard to law*, as respects obedience to whatever was for me the law of

[1] Col. ii. 11.   [2] Rom. xii. 1.   [3] *Verse* 4.   [4] *Verse* 5.

God, *a Pharisee*, a follower of *the most straitest sect of our religion*[1]*; in regard to zeal, a persecutor of the church*[2], carrying my zeal for God to the length of persecuting those whom I deemed in error; *in regard to righteousness, that* righteousness *which is in a law*, as respects that righteousness which a creature can find by strict obedience to that which is for him the law of his Creator, *become blameless*, one proved, or found, irreproachable in point of obedience.

Thus in every point, purity of descent from Abraham, strictness of ceremonial observance, warmth of zeal for God, and even consistency of moral uprightness, St Paul had everything upon which the most confident self-justifier could rely for salvation. And now the text tells us how he had learned to view it all

But whatsoever things were to me gains, these I have accounted for Christ's sake loss[3]. All the advantages enumerated above, advantages of birth, of character, and of ceremonial strictness, I have once for all cast away as not useless only but actually injurious. And this, *for the sake of Christ*, because they could not be retained with Christ, and because they were valueless without Christ Could not be retained, that is, as advantages, could not be relied upon, could not be trusted in, could not be reckoned as contributing anything to my hopes of acceptance and of salvation.

[1] Acts xxvi 5.   [2] *Verse 6.*   [3] *Verse 7.*

Is there not yet a little more than this in the words employed? Do they not say, that there was in all these things something of disadvantage, something of injury, as well as of non-advantage and of unprofitableness? Was there not in them a temptation to self-confidence and to self-righteousness, as well as an absence of help towards a Christian and an Evangelical trust?

The subject thus introduced will lead us to say a few plain words upon the Christian estimate of gain and loss The Christian man keeps an accurate account-book. He reckons up with intelligence and with an enlightened judgment his gains and his losses. And most important is it that those who would be Christian men should be rightly informed and rightly minded upon this great question, this question which takes precedence of other questions inasmuch as it is preliminary and introductory to all, What is gain to me, and what is loss?

I need not say what answer the world would return to this enquiry. And I need not say what answer the natural heart would return to this enquiry. And I need not say what answer the religion of many persons would return to this enquiry. Examine the accounts of nine-tenths of this congregation. See what items this man and that has entered on the side of gain, and what items on the side of loss There will be a marvellous agreement on this matter amongst those who agree on few matters. You will find health entered as a clear gain, and money as a clear gain; comfort, ease, tranquillity of mind and life, prosperity in business, a sufficient and a growing income, all these things will be found at once carried to the side of profit, and no hesitation, and no further question asked, concerning them. And you will as surely find sickness, disappointment, contraction of the means of pleasure, stagnation or decay of trade, the being outstripped by a rival in business, anxiety, sorrow, pain, bereavement, entered in the same reckoning as an undoubted and an unmixed loss. And when we come to matters bearing more directly upon the interests of the soul, we shall see that the natural heart has entered unhesitatingly on the side of gain, eternal gain, the respectability of an outward life, the preservation of a good character, punctuality (if it be so) in attendance upon Christian ordinances, and a conscience silent from all reproaches as to definite injuries committed against the bodies or the fortunes of neighbours and fellow-men. If the tablets of memory shew a fair record here, if respectability of life, if attention to natural duties, if propriety of speech and act, if reverence for God's name and attention to God's worship, can be pointed to as standing in fair array on the pages of that book of account; who is there who is not sometimes conscious of the rising boast, *God, I thank Thee that I am not as other men are*[1]*?* who is there who does not congratulate himself on having made sure of both worlds? who is there who, if he were laid on his deathbed in his present mind and feeling, would not say to his friend or his minister with something of complacency and self-satisfaction, *I know nothing against myself... I have wronged no man, I have defrauded no man...*I thank God that I am not afraid to die?

And never imagine, my brethren, that any minister rightly instructed in the truth of God will teach you to decry or to undervalue any one of these things. It is far better to have a good conscience than a bad one. It is far better to have no crime heavy upon your memory, than to see your own hand red with the blood of souls, souls neglected through your apathy, misled through your cruelty, or betrayed through your perfidy. We can have no fellow-feeling with those men who hold and avow the horrible maxim, The greater the sinner, the greater the saint. If in some notorious and in some more obscure instances God's great mercy has been vouchsafed to one who long had lived in sin, changing him as in a moment from a blasphemer and a profligate into a believer and a Christian, yet let us not forget the comparative rarity of such a transformation; let us not understate the fearful struggles through which that new birth is accomplished, and the yet more

[1] Luke xviii. 11.

fearful perils which beset the growth and the maturity; let us not imagine that the sin has in any manner helped the grace, even if, through God's wondrous mercy, *where sin abounded, grace did much more abound*[1].

Rather let us admit, for truth and holiness require it, that it is a gain to have been moral from the youth up. It is a gain, it must be so, never to have *known the depths of Satan*[2]. O from what experiences of guilty secrets, from what after-tastes of forbidden and nauseous fruits, from what snares and tendencies and habits too (in later and better days) of lingering corruption, does a blameless youth save a man! St Paul says not one word here of morality being a loss. He never says that his blameless life was a regret to him. He never says that he should have valued Christ more, had he been a greater sinner. Let no man so read his words, for so are they not written.

But this he says, and I would pray your deep attention to it, that for Christ's sake he now accounts as loss all that he had once accounted gain. He was an Israelite of direct descent from the father of the faithful: was that a loss? Would he have been a better man if he had been born a Gentile and an idolater? He had been blameless in his observance of God's ceremonial and (as he understood it) of God's moral law also: was that a loss? does he

[1] Rom. v. 20. [2] Rev. ii. 24.

regret that he had not habitually broken it? None of these things. The loss was, that he had been tempted to rest, and that he had rested, that he had been tempted to trust, and that he had trusted, in these possessions; in this purity of descent, in this scrupulosity of obedience. He had looked to them for salvation He had thought that God must be satisfied with so unexceptionable a genealogy, that God never could condemn so respectable, so diligent a worshipper. The reason why he calls his apparent gains a loss is, that they had too great a tendency to make him trust in them; to make him look to outward things as his passport to heaven, to make him build on a foundation of his own, and not upon the rock of another's righteousness.

And, my brethren, in this point of view, do not many of us need instruction, need warning? What are we trusting in? I know that some are putting off that question altogether. I know that some are saying in their hearts, I will live while I can, and die when I must...I will not torment myself before the time...I have some years before me yet...I shall do well enough, or else I must do as I may, when my change comes. But this childish recklessness, this suicidal infatuation, is not upon all of us. There are those who have a religion · and I ask them this day, earnestly and affectionately, what that religion is ? Is it much more than a moral life, and a punctual

Sunday worship? Is it much more than a doing one's duty, and a trusting in God's mercy? Good words, my brethren, excellent words, if they be but well used, if they be but spiritually discerned! But suffer me to ask you, Where is Christ in all this? What know you of the thought, *Things which were gains to me, these I have accounted for Christ's sake loss?* What of your own are you dismissing, discarding, trampling underfoot in order that you may rest in Christ alone? Where are your gains now become losses? Where are your transfers from the one side of your reckoning to the other because of Christ? I say it sorrowfully, but I say it with a deep sense of its truth, that many of us live and die on the strength of a Gospel which has no Christ in it; no demolition of self, whether in the form of self-confidence or of self-seeking, and no exaltation of Christ upon the ruins of self, either as our Saviour, or as our Lord. We are, at best, what St Paul was before his conversion What St Paul was—alas! let me say, St Paul without his good conscience, and St Paul without his accurate, scrupulous, devoted obedience.

Let not the words sound harshly in any ear. Why are they spoken? Is it not in the name of One who still and *ever liveth to make intercession*[1], and who has sent us as His own ambassadors praying you to be reconciled to God[2]? O if any of us feel that at

---

[1] Heb. vii. 25   [2] 2 Cor v 20

present our religion, our very Gospel, has practically no Christ in it, what can be so persuasive a summons to seek Him while we may, and to seek Him till we find? What can so solemnly yet so lovingly counsel us to lay afresh (if need be) the very foundations of our hope, before the last storm *ariseth to shake terribly the earth*[1]? There He stands, crucified and risen; dead once for sin, now alive again for ever; unseen, yet near; ready to listen, ready to save; shall we not come to Him, that we may have life[2]? He will cause breath to enter into the dry bones[3] of our withered and inanimate Gospel: He will make it once again, as in the days of old, instinct with life and power· yea, He will make Himself real to us as to His first disciples, and enable us by faith to look up stedfastly into heaven, and see Him, *the Son of man, standing on the right hand of God*[4].

[1] Isai. ii 21.   [2] John v 40.   [3] Ezek. xxxvii. 5.
[4] Acts vii 56

FIFTH SUNDAY AFTER THE EPIPHANY,
February 9, 1862.

LECTURE XIII.

PHILIPPIANS III. 8, 9.

8 *Nay rather, I even account all things to be loss, because of the superiority of the knowledge of Christ Jesus my Lord, for whose sake I was sentenced to the loss of all things, and*
9 *count them to be refuse, that I might gain Christ, and be found in Him, not having a righteousness of my own, that which is of a law, but that which is by means of faith in Christ, the righteousness which is of God on the ground of the faith.*

LECTURE XIII.

PHILIPPIANS III. 8, 9

That I may win Christ, and be found in Him.

WE have read, in a former verse, of a remarkable inversion of the common estimate of gain and loss. A Christian's accounts are kept in an opposite manner to those of the world. The two sides of his reckoning are reversed. What the world would call gain, he enters as loss: and what the world would enter as loss, he puts down as gain. It was the object of a former discourse to state and to apply this truth. It is not that a Christian takes that morbid view, which some have recommended, of this life and its blessings: he does not speak, as some have presumed to speak, of the misfortune of wealth, or the evil of talent, or the curse of health: in such language he sees nothing but unreality, nothing but distortion, nothing but ingratitude. Still there is a sense in which even these advantages are regarded by him as losses. Anything which has a tendency to draw him earthwards, to fix his thoughts and affections, his treasure and therefore also his heart[1], below, must be to him, if not an evil, yet at least a danger; and with regard to all these things he has need to watch and pray always, lest in his case those awful words should be verified, *I will curse your blessings*[2]....*Let the things that should have been for their wealth be unto them an occasion of falling*[3]. More especially is this true in regard to religious privileges. St Paul had found from experience how nearly allied are morality and self-righteousness; how much more nearly, ceremonial scrupulosity and the spirit of the Pharisee: and, though he never regrets that he had not been in earlier years an immoral man and a profligate, yet he did find it necessary to enter it on the side of loss in his reckoning, that he had once too much trusted in the purity of his descent, the strictness of his exclusiveness, and the punctuality of his observances *What things were gains to me, these I have accounted for Christ's sake loss.*

He goes on to say that he persists in this estimate, and carries it all lengths.

Nay rather, to speak more strongly and more correctly, *I even account all things to be loss*, not only those advantages which I have enumerated, but everything else that I have possessed or that I have been, *because of the superiority*, the surpassing

[1] Luke xii. 34.   [2] Mal. ii. 2.   [3] Ps. lxix. 22.

excellence, *of the knowledge of Christ Jesus my Lord*[1] Observe the appropriating word, *my Lord*. We all call Jesus Christ *our Lord:* which of us can say with St Paul, *my Lord?* which of us would not shrink from the responsibility involved in that appropriation, or from the retort which it might suggest, *If I be a master, where is my fear*[2]*?*

St Paul was not afraid of this. He could say, *The life which I now live in the flesh I live by the faith of the Son of God, who loved me and gave Himself for me*[3]. He could say, *I count all things but loss because of the surpassing excellence* in my regard *of the knowledge of Christ Jesus my Lord*.

For whose sake I was sentenced to the loss of all things. The expression is peculiar. It is taken from the proceedings of a court of justice. It denotes that sort of judicial sentence which subjects a man to the payment of a fine, or of what in some forms of procedure are called damages; a pecuniary penalty for some act proved against him. *For Christ's sake I was sentenced to the loss of all things*, of all that I had and of all that I was, every possession, every privilege, every advantage, every merit, every trust, and every boast.

And this as a single act. He refers this confiscation of his all to the moment when he became a Christian. When, after rising from the ground on

[1] *Verse* 8. [2] Mal. 1. 6. [3] Gal. 11. 20.

which he had fallen as Christ spoke to him from heaven, and after lying for three days in blindness and anguish in the house of Judas in Damascus[1], he heard at length from the lips of Ananias the words of peace and forgiveness, and obeyed the glad summons to *arise and be baptized, and wash away his sins, calling on the name of the Lord*[2]; there and then, in those baptismal waters through which he passed into the new life and new hopes of a Christian, he left behind him all the past; not more its habits and its prejudices, than its treasures of a self-made righteousness; not more its sin and its guilt than its prized possessions and its vaunted privileges. For Christ's sake he accepted this sweeping sentence, which stripped off all the past, and left him bare and naked and alone. His heart went along with this surrender. *For Christ's sake I was sentenced to the loss of all things, and I count them to be but filth or refuse.*

There must have been a motive for such submission. A man does not consent to loss but in the hope of gain. What was St Paul's object in consenting to the loss of his all?

That I might gain Christ, and be found in Him, not having a righteousness of my own, that which is of a law, that which results from obeying the law, whatever it be, of ceremonial or moral duty, *but that*

---

[1] Acts ix. 11.   [2] Acts xxii. 16.

which is by means of faith in Christ, the righteousness which is of God[1], of which God is the Author and Bestower, *on the ground of the faith*, that is, the Gospel; as the result of receiving and embracing the Gospel.

That I might gain Christ...That I might be found in Christ...these are the two parts of our subject.

1. St Paul has consented to the loss of all things; nay, he has transferred to the side of loss, in his accounts, all that once stood on the side of gain; and, if the matter stopped there, we might have pronounced him a bankrupt as much in hope as in possession. But he now says that he purposed to replace all his cancelled gains by one single item. On the side of loss we should find henceforth in his account-book a long list of forfeited and discarded advantages: we should find ease and comfort and reputation and honour; we should find membership of Israel, the straitness of the Pharisee, education under Gamaliel, zeal for God, the righteousness of an orthodox creed and of a burdensome ritual: page after page is crowded with the particulars of a departed hope and an obsolete trust. what is there to set against these losses? Just one word, just one name, a monosyllable, the name, as some would tell us, of a dead man[2], the name of One whom rulers and philosophers have agreed in rejecting and despising...*That I may gain CHRIST*.

[1] *Verse* 9.   [2] Acts xxv. 19.

The expression may remind us of one which the same Apostle has elsewhere employed, when he says, in writing to the Ephesians, *Unto me, who am less than the least of all saints, is this grace given, that I should preach among the Gentiles the unsearchable riches of Christ*[1]. When St Paul hoped to be able to write the word CHRIST on the side of his receipts, he hoped to enter there the brief summary of inexhaustible treasures, enough to counterbalance the loss of all things, and to replace it by an inestimable and incalculable gain.

And now let us drop the figure, and ask, so far as it is lawful for us to penetrate the strange secret, What was it which St Paul meant when he spoke of gaining Christ?

We might say, that he hoped for a share in Christ's atonement for sin, in Christ's intercession with God, in Christ's final sentence of acquittal, in Christ's summons into eternal glory. And St Paul did hope for each of these things. But does any one of them, do they all together, express what he meant when he wrote, *That I might gain Christ?* We answer readily that he meant something far more satisfying, far more personal, far more concentrated and combined. He meant one thing: yea, he meant one Person.

We would not willingly introduce that which shall

[1] Eph. iii. 8.

sound in any ear as fanciful or mystical. But we speak only the language of truth and soberness, of experience and of Scripture, when we say that the heart of man, of all men consciously or unconsciously, is hungering and thirsting for that which only a Person can satisfy; not hungering and thirsting for a gift, not hungering and thirsting for an influence, not hungering and thirsting for freedom from a felt evil or for possession of a desired good—even if that evil be the wrath of God, even if that good be God's forgiveness and God's absolution—but hungering and thirsting for the love of a Person; a Person who can be admired without the suspicion of exaggeration, adored without the risk of idolatry, trusted in without danger of disappointment, and reposed upon without the possibility of failure or of separation for ever. Hence the passionate longings, hence the bitter heart-griefs, hence the cruel anxieties, hence the disconsolate mournings, which make this earth a scene of disquiet and of unrest, and overspread many lives with a darkness which may be felt.

Do I address any this morning, who have had experience of the want thus described? Never can a hundred persons be gathered together, without there being present some whose life is poisoned at its source by this kind of misery. Surely for these above others, was the Gospel made just what it is. It had been beside the mark for these, if it had been ever so convincing in its intellectual arguments, or ever so elevating in its moral exhortations. What makes it a Gospel for these is its being the revelation of One who loves and may be loved; of One who is indeed the *chiefest among ten thousand* and *altogether lovely*[1]; of One who loved when we were sinners[2], and who sees of the travail of His soul[3] whensoever one sinner is brought to love Him. The Gospel of our salvation is the offer of a Person to be the strength of our hearts and our portion for ever[4]; of a God, who is Man also, to be as much the possession of each one of His redeemed as if that one were alone in the universe, and as if for him exclusively the scheme of redemption had been framed and the work of redemption accomplished.

That I may win...that I may gain Christ. How, my brethren, shall they who come to you as ambassadors from this Saviour plead with you in His behalf? Shall it not be by saying in His name to each restless, each dissatisfied, each roving heart, *Come unto Him, O thou that labourest, and art heavy laden, and He will give thee rest*[5]? Shall it not be by saying, Count all things else but loss if Christ may be won; and be assured that His love, sought, found, embraced, lived for, will soften every disappointment, calm every

---

[1] Cant v. 10, 16.
[2] Rom v. 8.
[3] Isai. liii. 11.
[4] Ps. lxxiii 26.
[5] Matt. xi. 28.

anxiety, and *make your wilderness like Eden and your desert like the garden of the Lord*[1]*?*

Above all, be not induced to represent to yourselves as a thing altogether future the acquisition here described. St Paul does not say that he hopes to gain Christ hereafter, at a late point in this life, or in the world beyond death. He had submitted to the loss of all things, that he might gain Christ now. From the moment when that choice was made, he gained Christ. From that time forth he had Christ for his Friend, for his Saviour, for his Guide, for his Life. When he was in distress, *the Lord stood by him*[2], and spoke with him *as a man speaketh unto his friend*[3]. When he was under temptation, he applied to Christ for strength, and found that *strength made perfect in his weakness*[4]. When he was in danger, Christ breathed peace into his soul, and taught him that, whether living or dying, he was His; that *to depart and to be with Him*, whenever it was appointed, would be *far better*[5]. Above all, in whatever state he was, he had Christ present in him by His Spirit, and could say, *It is no longer I that live, but Christ liveth in me*[6]. In these and in suchlike experiences, the words of the text were already verified to him in one part, *That I might gain Christ.* God grant to each one of us, my brethren, to seek as he sought, and to find as he found!

[1] Isai. li. 3.
[2] Acts xxiii. 11.
[3] Ex xxxiii. 11.
[4] 2 Cor. xii. 9.
[5] Phil. i. 23
[6] Gal. ii. 20.

Let this be the special aim of each one of us who kneels this morning before Christ's Table. If there has been anything heretofore of unreality, at least of impersonality, in our thoughts concerning Him; if we have thought rather of His atonement than of Himself, if we have been satisfied to ask God for forgiveness through what He has done, rather than to ask God to reveal Him in us by His Spirit[1]; let us use His holy ordinance this day as an opportunity of rising to a more direct and a more personal communication with Him as He now is in heaven, asking Him to be to us that which He once was to His Apostles St Paul or St John, a loving and loved, a living and lifegiving Person, that we may in no long time be able to say from our hearts, *I have won Christ...I have found Christ*

2. This at present. This in the life that is. But the eye of the Christian is not bounded in its range. He looks yet beyond, to the day of his departure, to the day of Christ's coming, to the hour of death and to the day of judgment. And St Paul's second aim is directed to that great day. That I may win Christ, *and be found in Him.*

Suppose the day come. Suppose the human creation, risen from death[2], or changed instantaneously into the likeness of the risen[3], awaiting that last scrutiny which is to decide eternity. Alas! *who may*

[1] Gal. i. 16.   [2] John v. 28, 29.   [3] 1 Cor xv. 51.

abide the day of His coming? and who shall stand when He appeareth[1]*?* Can human merit, can blamelessness (as man speaks) of life, can the fulfilment of relative duties, can that righteousness which is of the law, furnish a sufficient screen and shelter in that day of omniscient search, of revelation of motives, of exposure of hearts[2]? How much less still can the open sinner, the profane and the impure, abide that ordeal! The avenger of blood[3] is behind: where is that city of refuge which can avail anything then?

The second half of the text has special reference to that day. St Paul had submitted to the loss of all things now, in the hope that he might be safe then. While others shall be found in that day standing as it were exposed and defenceless while God's judgments are abroad upon the earth, even like those Egyptians of old, who believed not the prediction of the plague of hail, and dared its perils in the open field[4], St Paul, and those who like him and with him have believed, will then not be exposed, not be unsheltered—they will be *found in Christ.* When the avenger looks for me, I shall not be seen, I shall not be discovered: he will look for me, and he will find only Christ. I shall be inside that refuge against which God's own judgment shall have no power. Judgment may seek me, but I shall not be to be found; only Christ, only the

---

[1] Mal. iii. 2.   [2] 1 Cor. iv. 5.   [3] Nu. xxxv. 27.
[4] Ex. ix. 21.

Saviour, only the Judge[1]. Could any words express more forcibly the safety of the Christian? He will be found enclosed, incorporated, and thus hidden, in Christ Himself, in the Lord, in the Judge, of man! *It is God that justifieth: who is he that condemneth*[2]*?*

My brethren, may God in His mercy save us, as from despair, so also from a false hope! If we would be found in Christ then, we must gain Him now. Ill will it be for that man whose personal knowledge of Christ has to begin in the day of judgment. O that we might be wise in time! What is it which keeps us back from winning Christ now? Let each one ask himself, What keeps me back? Which of those *all things* which St Paul thought it worth while to sacrifice? Is it carelessness? is it lightness of mind? is it procrastination? is it a habit of trifling? is it worldliness? is it the fear of man? is it the love of things perishable and temporal? is it the lust of gain? is it the predominance of some bosom sin? is it a reliance upon my own morality, my punctuality of worship, my right dealing towards all men? O look into your own heart: see it as God sees it: see it as it is: see it as you must one day see it: and postpone not the enquiry until it be too late, until conscience

---

[1] See *Expository Sermons* by the late Rev. E. T. Vaughan, M.A. Vicar of St Martin's, Leicester (published by Crossley and Clark, Leicester, 1843), page 374, &c.

[2] Rom. viii. 33, 34.

be seared, until the will be enfeebled, until habit have become law, until sin finished have brought forth death! *Seek ye the Lord while He may be found*[1] *The night cometh, when no man can work*[2].

[1] Isai. lv. 6.   [2] John ix. 4

QUINQUAGESIMA SUNDAY,
    March 2, 1862.

LECTURE XIV.

PHILIPPIANS III 10, 11.

10 For the sake of knowing Him, and the power of His resurrection, and the fellowship of His sufferings, being
11 (*gradually*) conformed to His death, if by any means I might arrive at the resurrection from among the dead

LECTURE XIV.

PHILIPPIANS III. 10.

That I may know Him, and the power of His resurrection.

ST Paul is still speaking of the hope and the purpose which he entertained when he became a Christian. More especially, of that hope and that purpose under the influence of which he consented to that entire confiscation of his previous possessions, both outward and spiritual, which accompanied his entrance upon the Christian life. *But whatsoever things were to me gains, these I have considered for Christ's sake loss*[1]. *Nay rather, I even consider all things to be loss, on account of the superiority of the knowledge of Christ Jesus my Lord, for whose sake I suffered the loss of all things,* was sentenced as it were to forfeit my all, *and consider them to be but refuse, in order that I might gain Christ*[2], *and be found in Him, not having a*

[1] Verse 7. [2] Verse 8

righteousness of my own, that which is of a law, that sort of righteousness which springs out of obedience to a rule of duty, *but that which is by means of faith in Christ, the righteousness which is of God*[1], which springs out of God, which is God's gift and God's work alone, *on the ground of the faith*, that is, the Gospel.

And then follow the words of the text; depending, you will perceive, upon this clause, *For whose sake I was sentenced to the loss of my all, and consider it but refuse.*

He has said before that this was submitted to in order that he *might gain Christ and be found in Him*, in the sense explained on a former occasion. Now he expresses the same truth in a slightly different form.

For the sake of knowing Him, and the power of His resurrection, and the fellowship of His sufferings, being gradually conformed to His death[2], *if by any means I might arrive at* (*reach* or *attain to*) *the resurrection of the dead;* or more precisely, *the resurrection which is from among dead men*[3].

The latter part of this most important passage I purpose to consider in the evening: to the few words read as the text we will seriously and earnestly address ourselves now. *I submitted to the forfeiture and confiscation of my all*, to the loss of position and reputation, of privilege and boasting, of a fancied

[1] *Verse* 9.   [2] *Verse* 10   [3] *Verse* 11.

security and a self-constructed righteousness, *for the sake of knowing Christ, and the power of His resurrection.*

You will observe, in the very outset, that there is but one way of really knowing Christ—whatever that expression may denote—namely, the parting with everything else. More particularly, the parting with every remnant and vestige of self-confidence and self-righteousness. I do not suppose that there is any one here present who really thinks himself perfect, who does not confess that in many things he is faulty and even sinful; certainly there is no one here this morning who has not told his God, in the course of this service, that he is a miserable sinner, a miserable offender, and that there is no health in him. But, alas! *the heart is deceitful...who can know it*[1]*?* and I fear there may be many such confessions duly made through a long lifetime, without one spark of genuine humility or of true self-abasement. And therefore I would repeat it—in the hope that God may bless the word to some one soul now before Him—that our only way to the knowledge of Christ, like St Paul's way to the knowledge of Christ, lies through a total forfeiture and confiscation of every other hope and of every other trust. God grant that, if we should ever be called to minister beside the deathbed of one of those who are worshipping here

[1] Jer. xvii 9.

in health and strength to-day, we may not be pained by hearing any of those miserable fallacies with which Satan deludes so many at that solemn hour— I thank God I have a good conscience...I have nothing to make me afraid to meet God...I am not one of those who have cause to fear death! God grant that we may be enabled to lay a stronger foundation[1] than that for the house of our eternal hopes!

St Paul, a better man than any of us, had found the hollowness of all self-trust. He had willingly consented to part with all that he had once thought most valuable, in a religious sense, *for the sake of knowing Christ, and the power of His resurrection.*

1. *For the sake of knowing Christ.* The expression will remind us of our Lord's own saying, in His prayer to the Father, as recorded in the 17th chapter of St John's Gospel: *This is life eternal, that they might know Thee the only true God, and Jesus Christ whom Thou hast sent*[2]. *This is life eternal:* the strength of the expression will show us why St Paul spoke so earnestly of his desire to know Christ. In that knowledge, he was aware, lay his eternal life.

I think it quite needless to caution any one now amongst us against the error of understanding these words of a merely intellectual knowledge of Christ If that were all, it would not be an equivalent for that which St Paul had given up for it. *Thou believest*

[1] Luke vi. 48.   [2] John xvii 3

that there is one God: thou doest well: the devils also believe, and tremble[1]. Thou knowest that there is a Christ: thou doest well: the devils also believe, and tremble. When He was upon earth, unclean spirits often spoke to Him by human lips, and said, *I know Thee who Thou art, the Holy One of God*[2]. And the merciful Saviour derived no satisfaction from that confession On the contrary, He rebuked the utterance: *He suffered not*, St Mark tells us, according to the marginal version of the words, *the devils to say that they knew Him*[3]. It was painful and shocking to His holy nature, to hear the avowal of a conviction so vain and so compulsory. And do not you think that it would pain Him now to hear some of us say, *I believe in Jesus Christ? Thou art the King of glory, O Christ?* Might He not say to some of us, It were better for you not to know me? Might He not say, What profiteth a man such knowledge, except he also use it and live by it?

Such knowledge as this St Paul might have acquired without parting with his all to gain it. Let us compare it with that which he here speaks of.

And we would say, first, that though the intellectual knowledge of Christ is not the whole nor the chief part of man's great need, yet it must not be undervalued We may have it, and yet be nothing

[1] James ii. 19. [2] Mark i. 24, Luke iv. 34.
[3] Mark i. 34; Luke iv. 41.

profited, but, on the other hand, without it the other cannot be. A man must know of Christ by the hearing of the ear[1], if he would ever know Him for himself by faith. *How shall they believe,* St Paul himself asks, *in Him of whom they have not heard*[2]*?* And let me say more than this: there are many persons, acquainted with the name and elementary doctrine of Christ, who are kept back from a saving approach to Him by not knowing more of Him: there are those whose hearts are never drawn to Him, chiefly because they do not study Him as He is described and revealed to us in the Gospel. O it is often the neglect of the Bible, as a book to be read and pondered and handled, which prevents men from admiring Christ, from desiring Christ, from seeking and finding Him. St Paul evidently thought much of doctrine. He was diligent in making out all that he could of Christ. Every saying which was reported by those who had been on earth *eye-witnesses and ministers of the Word*[3], was caught and treasured up by him with an eager fondness. And every truth which he himself received from Christ as a part of the revelation committed to his Apostleship, was communicated by him with a scrupulous fidelity to the Churches which he planted. *I have received of the Lord that which also I delivered unto you*[4]*...I delivered*

---

[1] Job xlii. 5.   [2] Rom. x. 14.   [3] Luke i. 2.
[4] 1 Cor. xi. 23.

unto you first of all that which I also received[1]... *Remember ye not, that, when I was yet with you, I told you these things*[2]? Yes, my brethren, if we loved Christ more, we should be more diligent students of His sayings. And is not the converse also true— that, if we studied His words and His acts more diligently, we should grow into a greater love of Him?

But doubtless, when St Paul wrote the words, *that I might know Him*, he had before his mind a different stage, we might say a different kind, of knowledge from this. He did not mean, and he does not say, *that I might know all about Christ*, but *that I might know Him*. The knowledge of which he speaks is a personal knowledge. It is a knowledge which presupposes intellectual knowledge, but which is something else. It is a knowledge to which the other is preliminary, introductory, subordinate, supplementary It is the knowledge of which we speak when we say of a man, I know him. What do we mean when we say this of a man? Do we not mean, I have seen him—I have observed him—I have conversed with him—I have interchanged thoughts with him—I have spent time with him—I have done things with him—in presence, I have been admitted to his confidence—in absence, I have written to him and heard from him? These things, and such as these, are what

---

[1] 1 Cor. xv. 3.   [2] 2 Thess. ii. 5.

make up personal knowledge between man and man. We should never say, I know such or such a great man of history—I know Alexander, or I know Cæsar, or I know Napoleon—merely because we have read of them, and could give an account of their exploits. We should not say this even of the great men of our own day, its statesmen, or generals, or philosophers— no, not even if we had seen them in public, or heard them speak, or read their writings—unless also we had been admitted to their society, and had exchanged with them the confidences which a man gives his friend. Even thus is it with the knowledge of Christ We have no right to say, I know Christ, merely because we have read of Him in Scripture, or because He has *taught in our streets*[1]. We have no right to say, I know Christ, unless He has often spoken to us and we to Him. Unless we have access to His privacy, and can tell Him our secrets. Unless we can go in and out where He dwells, and talk with Him as a man talketh with his friend. Unless we have not only read in Scripture that He is wise and merciful, powerful and long-suffering, but have also acted upon that information, and found Him so for ourselves. Unless in temptation we have cried to Him, and received strength: unless in trouble we have had recourse to Him, and our soul has been refreshed· unless in difficulty we have applied to

---

[1] Luke xiii. 26.

Him, and experienced a very present help, a very real direction It was for the sake of this sort of knowledge of Christ, for the sake of knowing Him personally and enjoying the privilege of His acquaintance and His friendship, for the sake of knowing Him in a manner which it would be presumptuous for me to pretend to describe to you, but which he has himself stated to us, expressly and incidentally, in his own letters to his friends and Epistles to his churches, that St Paul had thought it worth while to consent to the loss of all things, and to pour contempt on all his gain.

We will close this part of our subject by recalling two or three examples, from his own writings, of the sort of knowledge of Christ which St Paul enjoyed in this life

i The first is an example of the way in which his acquaintance with Christ reconciled him to the painful vicissitudes of outward circumstances.

Not that I speak in respect of want: for I have learned, in whatsoever state I am, therewith to be content I know both how to be abased, and I know how to abound: everywhere and in all things I am instructed both to be full and to be hungry, both to abound and to suffer need. I can do all things through Christ which strengtheneth me [1].

ii. The second is an example of the way in

[1] Phil iv. 11—13.

which his acquaintance with Christ brought him help under the emergencies of special danger.

At my first answer no man stood with me, but all men forsook me: I pray God that it may not be laid to their charge. Notwithstanding the Lord stood with me, and strengthened me...and I was delivered out of the mouth of the lion. And the Lord shall deliver me from every evil work, and will preserve me unto His heavenly kingdom: to whom be glory for ever and ever[1].

iii. The third is an example of the way in which his acquaintance with Christ brought him support and comfort amidst the special inward trials of his personal life.

Lest I should be exalted above measure through the abundance of the revelations, there was given to me a thorn in the flesh, the messenger of Satan to buffet me, lest I should be exalted above measure. For this thing I besought the Lord thrice, that it might depart from me. And He said unto me, My grace is sufficient for thee: for my strength is made perfect in weakness. Most gladly therefore will I rather glory in my infirmities, that the power of Christ may rest upon me ...for when I am weak, then am I strong[2].

Happy are the people that are in such a case: yea, blessed are the people who have the Lord for their God[3]*!*

---

[1] 2 Tim. iv 16—18.   [2] 2 Cor. xii 7—10.
[3] Ps. cxliv 15

2. The second clause of the text suggests to us a profitable addition to the thought presented in the former. For the sake of knowing Christ, *and the power of His resurrection*.

It is scarcely necessary to say that the meaning is not so much the power shewn in His resurrection, the manifestation of God's almighty strength in raising Christ from the dead, but rather the power with which resurrection invested Christ; that power upon which He entered as the result and consequence of His resurrection; that power which He still exercises throughout heaven and earth as the risen and exalted Saviour, as *He that liveth and was dead, and, behold, He is alive for evermore, and hath the keys of hell and of death*[1]. *All power is given unto me in heaven and in earth...and, lo, I am with you alway, even unto the end of the world*[2] The power of His *resurrection* might be expressed perhaps most intelligibly in the form, *His resurrection power*.

St Paul then declares that he had parted willingly with his all, for the sake of knowing Christ, and the power of Christ, not as exercised when He was a man upon earth, but as exercised after death, after resurrection, after ascension, in that state, in short, in which He still is after eighteen centuries more have run their course. *That I might know Him, and His resurrection power*.

[1] Rev. i 18.   [2] Matt. xxviii. 18, 20.

This is that power which the same Apostle describes when he speaks of *the life of Jesus*, His life, that is, now in heaven, being *made manifest in his body...made manifest in his mortal flesh*[1]; and gives this as the explanation of his endurance of afflictions and sufferings, such as must otherwise have overborne and crushed him. This is that power of which our Lord Himself, in the anticipation of His speedy entrance into His glory, said, in His last discourse to the disciples, *Because I live, ye shall live also*[2]. What can explain the mystery of a Christian's life on earth —*troubled* oftentimes *on every side, yet not distressed— perplexed, but not in despair—persecuted, but not forsaken—cast down, but not destroyed*[3]—save this truth, this fact, of the *resurrection power* of Christ? In himself, he is but as other men are, weak, irresolute, unstable, fallen: in his circumstances, inward and outward, he is often tried beyond other men: the devil plies every craft and every assault for his overthrow: sometimes he says, It is in vain—I cannot resist—I must sin, if I die for it and, unlike other men, he has the world too against him, rejoicing when he falters, triumphant when he falls· what can be less promising, what can be more alarming, than his position below? how is it that he escapes at all? how is it that, if you watch him in the conflict, he is

---

[1] 2 Cor. iv. 10, 11.   [2] John xiv. 19.
[3] 2 Cor. iv. 8, 9.

still armed, still erect, still combating—and if you see him at its close, he is *more than conqueror*[1]? how is it that, on the whole, though with many imperfections, his testimony on earth is for God, his garments are kept from foul stains, or else *washed and made white*, by deep repentance, *in the blood of the Lamb*[2]? These things could not be—yes, we say it in all truth and soberness, these things could not be — were it not for the *resurrection power* of his Saviour. Because He lives, His servants live: the risen life of Jesus is daily manifested in their body[3]. When they cry to Him, He hears them; when they are in trouble, He refreshes them; when they begin to sink, He stretches forth the sustaining hand; when they say, *Lord, save me, I perish*[4], He is ready to give the succour asked of Him, even if He adds together with it the gracious and comforting remonstrance, *O thou of little faith, wherefore didst thou doubt*[5]? And at last, when death comes, He who first Himself *tasted death for every man*[6] is ready with the sympathy which is strength also; *Yea, though I walk through the valley of the shadow of death, I will fear no evil; for Thou art with me; Thy rod and Thy staff they comfort me*[7].

My brethren, have we as yet any knowledge at

[1] Rom. viii. 37.   [2] Rev vii 14.   [3] 2 Cor. iv 10.
[4] Matt. viii. 25.   [5] Matt xiv. 31.   [6] Heb. ii. 9.
[7] Ps. xxiii 4.

all of the thing spoken of, of the power of Christ's resurrection? It is there; it is present; it is offered; it is yours: but you have thought scorn of it; you have not tried it; you have thought that your own strength would do for you; or you have looked this way and that for strength, and have missed the help which is absolutely almighty, certainly available. Let the words now spoken be, by God's mercy, the beginning to you of a new life! Say to yourself, Christ is; He was dead, He is alive again; He is as near to me as the soul of man is to the body· faith is the hand which touches Him, prayer is the voice which moves Him· who told me that I am not within the scope of His operation, within the reach of His risen power? I too will call upon Him, call upon Him in prosperity, call upon Him in health, call upon Him in happiness, or else, if the case be so, call upon Him in trouble, call upon Him in sickness, call upon Him in temptation· perhaps He will listen, perhaps He will help, perhaps He will save: seeking Him, none ever perished; waiting for Him, none ever was cast out. So may it be with me! *The promise may be yet for an appointed time; but at the end it shall speak, and not lie: though it tarry, I will wait for it; because it will surely come, it will not tarry* [1].

[1] Hab ii 3

SECOND SUNDAY IN LENT,
March 16, 1862

LECTURE XV.

PHILIPPIANS III 10, 11.

10 *For the sake of knowing **Him**, and the power of **His** resurrection, and the fellowship of **His** sufferings, being*
11 *(gradually) conformed to **His** death, if by any means I might arrive at the resurrection from among the dead.*

LECTURE XV.

PHILIPPIANS III. 10.

That I may know Him...and the fellowship of His sufferings.

THAT *I might know Him...and the power of His resurrection*, was our subject this morning; *that I might know Him and the fellowship of His sufferings*, is reserved for consideration this evening. To *gain Christ* St Paul had consented to the loss of all things. This *gaining* of Christ is afterwards expressed in the form of *knowing* Christ. And the knowledge spoken of—if only because it is equivalent to gaining Christ —cannot be a mere intellectual knowledge, such as all men have or might have, of the history of Christ, or of the mystery of His person, or of the qualities of His character, or of His will and purposes towards mankind. None of these things, nor all of them together, could make it worth while for St Paul to have parted with everything else that he might acquire them. Nor indeed are any or all of these things what we mean when we speak of knowing a person We mean something widely different. We mean something which is made up of communication and intercourse, of access and intimacy, of interchange of ideas and experience of sympathy. That sort of knowledge then is what St Paul in becoming a Christian hoped to have of Christ. When he made that momentous choice, fixed, we may suppose, during those three days of solitude and blindness[1], of deep thought and great searchings of heart, which followed upon his arrest by Christ Jesus on the way to Damascus; when he came to the resolution of giving his new convictions entire mastery over his life, and of sacrificing without one backward look every possession and every boast which could militate against them; he did so, he here tells us, in the hope that thus he should come to know Christ; to be admitted to His intimacy; to go in and out as he would in communication and communion with Him; and to find rest for his soul, and strength for his heart, and direction for his life, in that new, that Divine friendship. I willingly submitted to the forfeiture of all things, that I might know Christ.

He adds two particulars respecting this knowledge The knowledge for which he looked was a personal knowledge. The voice which had spoken to him in

---

[1] Acts ix 9

the way was the voice of a Person: *I am Jesus whom thou persecutest*[1]. That was the Person whom St Paul determined at every cost to know, to have for his friend, for the sharer of his thoughts, for the guide of his actions But there were two particular things for which he looked in this knowledge of Christ. First, he hoped to know *the power of His resurrection;* to become personally acquainted with that power with which His resurrection invested Him; a power universal and yet minute, a power which upholds all things and directs all things in heaven and earth, and which yet stoops to undertake the charge, even as if it had no other, of one single, sinful, feeble, erring and straying soul. St Paul hoped to experience this *resurrection power* of Christ within himself. He hoped to find it taking charge of him. He hoped (and he tells us that it was so) to perceive a power working in him—in every chance and change of human circumstance, in every variation and fluctuation of human feeling—of such efficacy, of such support, of such persuasiveness, of such sweetness, that nothing should ever overbear him, nothing should ever come amiss to him, nothing should ever separate him from a Father's love and from a Saviour's presence. *Because I live, ye shall live also*[2].

Thus far we have proceeded St Paul hoped to know Christ *and the power of His resurrection.*

[1] Acts ix 5. [2] John xiv. 19.

And now he adds that he hoped, when he became a Christian, to know Christ *and the fellowship of His sufferings, being conformed*—and the original expression indicates a gradual process, *being gradually conformed—to His death, if by any means I might arrive at the resurrection from among the dead.*

A few brief words of explanation will prepare us for carrying home what is here written

To be *conformed* to the death of Christ, is to be assimilated to, to be made to resemble His death ; to be made to bear the form or likeness of His death ; in other words, to be made like Christ in His death The parallel passage in the Epistle to the Romans will occur to many of you. *Know ye not that all we who were baptized into Christ Jesus were baptized into His death ? We were buried then with Him by means of our baptism, into His death; that even as Christ was raised from among the dead by the glory*, the manifested excellence, that is, the almighty power, *of the Father, so we also might walk*, might move and act, might exercise every function of our earthly being, *in newness of life*, in a new state of which the characteristic is life, spiritual, heavenly, eternal life *For if we have become of one nature with the likeness of His death, then shall we be also* of one nature with the likeness *of His resurrection: knowing this, that our old man*, our original self, the fallen sinful being in each one of us, *was crucified with Him, that the body of sin might be destroyed, that we might no longer be slaves of sin: for he that has died is* by that very fact *set free from sin. And if we died with Christ, we believe that we shall also live with Him...So do ye also reckon yourselves to be dead men with regard to sin, and living men with regard to God in Christ Jesus*[1]. Be like Christ in His death: have as little to do with sin as if you had already died, as if your body were in its grave, incapable of word or act of sin. That is the brief account of *being conformed*, as St Paul here expresses it, *to the death of Christ*.

And if this be so, then the resurrection of Christ shall be yours also. *Being gradually conformed to His death, if by any means*—the words themselves express the greatness, the difficulty, apart from God the impossibility, of the attainment—*if by any means I might reach the resurrection from among the dead*. See the place which the resurrection occupied in St Paul's doctrine, in St Paul's personal hopes! It was not death, it was not the intermediate state, not the Paradise of the blessed, not the immortality of the soul, for which he longed and to which he aspired: it was the consummation of all these things in the resurrection of the just. Not until then shall the adoption be complete; not until the redemption of the soul has been perfected by the redemption of the body. O how far have we fallen from the fulness

[1] Rom. vi. 3—11.

and from the simplicity, and from the liveliness of the apostolic doctrine, of the primitive hope!

And now after this brief glance at a vast subject, into which the time forbids us to enter at present more deeply, we must concentrate all our attention, God helping us, upon the very words of the text; *that I may know Christ...and the fellowship of His sufferings.*

St Paul, in becoming a Christian, hoped in general to know Christ, and hoped in particular to know two things; the power of Christ's resurrection, and the fellowship of Christ's sufferings He desired to experience in himself, day by day, the power of the risen Saviour; and he hoped to realize in himself, day by day, the fellowship of His sufferings. In other words, to be enabled patiently and even thankfully to endure that condition of suffering, inward and outward, which Christ Himself when He was upon earth had borne before him.

Very remarkable in every point of view is the hope thus expressed. It was St Paul's ambition to share Christ's sufferings. It was not a thing which he must submit to, in order to a greater good. He represents it, rather, as one of two chief and coordinate objects; the knowledge of the resurrection power of Christ, and the knowledge of a share in Christ's sufferings.

It is thus that he expresses himself to the Colossians, when he says, *I rejoice in my sufferings for you, and fill up that which is behind,* that which is still lacking, *of the afflictions of Christ in my flesh for His body's sake which is the Church*[1]. It was as if Christ's own sufferings had still to be completed in the sufferings of His disciples; as if even that sacred life of constant buffeting and constant privation had not exhausted the cup of sorrow, but had left some dregs at the bottom of it for His people to wring out. It is thus also that he writes to the Corinthians in his second Epistle, in a passage already more than once quoted to-day, *Always bearing about in the body the dying of the Lord Jesus, that the life also of Jesus might be made manifest in our body For we which live are alway delivered unto death for Jesus' sake, that the life also of Jesus might be made manifest in our mortal flesh*[2] And thus St Peter also bids the Church not to *think it strange concerning the fiery trial which is to try them*...but rather to *rejoice, inasmuch as they are partakers of Christ's sufferings*[3]. All these passages speak the same language: he who would win Christ, he who would know Christ, must expect, must be willing, nay, must be even desirous, not only to know the power of His resurrection, but to know also by experience the fellowship of His sufferings. *It is a faithful saying; If we died with Him, we shall also live with Him: if we suffer (endure), we shall also*

[1] Col 1. 24.   [2] 2 Cor. IV. 10, 11.   [3] 1 Pet. IV. 12, 13.

reign with Him[1]. St Paul was not willing only, he was desirous, to know not one only but both of these things.

Now therefore, my brethren, let us take fully into view the condition to which we are called. Let us regard it with firm and steady eye, until at last, like this great Apostle, we even grow into the love of it. The Christian life is not a triumphant, still less is it a secure and confident progress along a path strewn with flowers or levelled into smoothness. Every single Christian must, in some way or other, be a partaker in Christ's sufferings. The allotments of suffering, like the gifts of grace, are various indeed, perhaps unequal; but in kind, if not in degree, all must expect to taste all, each must expect to taste each, and the very power of Christ's resurrection will be chiefly shewn in supporting His servants through the fellowship of His sufferings. It is in *bearing about the dying of the Lord Jesus*, that *the life also of Jesus*[2], His risen life, is chiefly manifested and chiefly felt.

There are two principal departments in which this fellowship of suffering is realized; in relation to pain, and in relation to sin. It may be that St Paul wrote mainly of the former; and it may be that we require to think mainly of the latter.

I   There is a fellowship of Christ's sufferings in

[1] 2 Tim. ii. 11, 12.   [2] 2 Cor. iv. 10.

relation to pain. How beautifully is this drawn out in our Service for the Visitation of the Sick! *There should be no greater comfort to Christian persons, than to be made like unto Christ, by suffering patiently adversities, troubles, and sicknesses. For He Himself went not up to joy, but first He suffered pain: He entered not into His glory, before He was crucified. So truly our way to eternal joy is to suffer here with Christ; and our door to enter into eternal life is gladly to die with Christ, that we may rise again from death, and dwell with Him in everlasting life*[1].

The pains of life, inward and outward, are as various as the bodies and the souls upon which they fasten. Our sensibilities to pain are very various: one thing hurts one person, and another another: that which is agony to me, my neighbour scarcely feels This is true of the roughnesses of life, and it is true of the calumnies of life, and it is true of the disappointments of life. It is true of those trials which come to us through the affections, and it is true of those trials which come to us through the ambitions, of our nature On the whole, the varieties of constitutional sensibility are least seen, though they are seen, in reference to bodily suffering One bears bravely, and another shrinks at the first access of pain: but the actual torture, however differently endured, is felt in some measure by all. And let us

[1] Exhortation, *part* 2.

add that those to whom sorrow and suffering do not come, often go in quest of them. they have self-made troubles, as hard to endure as those which God sends upon us : nay, there is this, at least, of visible compensation in the matter of pain, that real suffering drives out the imaginary, and that where the lot is one of outward want or of physical anguish, there by the very nature of the case the distresses of mere sentiment are excluded, and the woes of a wounded spirit driven into the far distance.

Thus much we may say with certainty, that no man, and therefore no Christian, passes through life untouched by distress. The cause may vary, and the kind may vary, and the degree may vary, all but infinitely; still the fact is there, the thing is there; the experience must be gained, as alone it can be gained, through suffering; and oftentimes the even tenour of an untroubled life, in its brightest and serenest day, is but *the torrent's smoothness ere it dash below.*

But in all this there is lacking as yet the essential feature of a fellowship in Christ's sufferings. Alas! of the thousands and tens of thousands for whom life is at this moment a time of unspeakable bitterness, how many, think you, are suffering with Christ? For this, faith is needful, and devotion is needful, and submission is needful, and the support of a heavenly arm, and the expectation of a heavenly home: and where almost amongst us are these things? unless it be in the fevered visions of the very last hours, when surrounding friends catch a ray of hope from a few half-conscious words, strangely at variance (could they but see it) with the general tenour of the now closing life.

St Paul's meaning, when he wrote the words *the fellowship of His sufferings*, was something far different from all these things. His life was Christ. To Him he had devoted first himself, and then his all. All his desires, all his interests, all his objects, were swallowed up in this one, the living to Christ's glory; the so living as to make men know Christ, and love Christ, and serve Christ, as their one happiness and their one hope. It was in this sort of life that trouble met him. It was in the sacrifice of life to this work that he met want and scorn and desertion, watchings and fastings, stripes and imprisonments[1], at last death itself. O my brethren, what becomes of us when we drag ourselves into this comparison? Where is our work for Christ, our devotion to Christ, our sacrifice for Christ, our life hidden, merged, lost in Him? Let us think of this question: and if we can do no great things, and suffer no great things, in His behalf, at least let us see that common life is lived in the remembrance of Him, life's pleasures subordinated to His will, life's anxieties, sorrows, and sicknesses, endured patiently in His strength.

[1] 2 Cor vi. 5

2 Yet more entirely may we enter into the fellowship of Christ's sufferings, when we turn, in the second and last place, from the thought of pain to the thought of sin. *In that He died*, St Paul writes, *He died unto sin once*[1]. His sufferings were not merely exemplary, they were propitiatory too. *By His stripes we are healed. The chastisement of our peace was upon Him*[2]. When He suffered, it was not only at the hand of sinners, it was also for the obliteration of the sinner's sin. Now in that highest of all senses we cannot share His sufferings. We cannot, and thank God, we need not. He has done all. We can add nothing. But that conflict with sin, with its assaults and with its wiles, with its contradictions and its perversenesses, with its temptations and its infirmities, which He waged throughout His earthly life within and without, that conflict which was the main cause of His being *a Man of sorrows*[3], and of which (in one of its most marked seasons) we are now keeping the annual commemoration, in that conflict we may all have a share; in that conflict every one of Christ's servants has had and must have his share; and in that participation lies for us the chief part of the solemn lesson of the text, when it bids us seek, bids us aspire to the knowledge of Christ and of the fellowship of His sufferings.

Need I say to any one who hears me that there is

[1] Rom. vi. 10.   [2] Isai. liii. 5.   [3] Isai. liii. 3.

suffering in that conflict? So long as we are contented to talk of Christian life in general terms, of sin in the abstract, and duty in the abstract, so long there is no place for suffering. Why should the enemy alarm by opposition those who are his already by surrender? But do I speak to none this night who have gone far beyond this? to none who have buckled on the Divine armour and fought many a battle with the hosts of evil within them? I will bring the matter lower down and closer home. Are there none here who have had to do desperate battle with a besetting sin? none who have had within their bosom a lurking passion, unsuspected perhaps by man, but threatening them—and they knew it— with utter ruin, with the damnation of hell? And did they set themselves vigorously in Christ's strength to conquer this foe? O they can tell a tale of suffering I well know, in that obscure, that most secret warfare! They can tell how dreadful it is never to have a moment's security; never to know what it is to lie down or to rise up without fear of an enemy in the very camp, in the very citadel, of their being. They can tell what a victory cost them in that strife; what an agony of earnestness, what mortifying of the will, what crucifixion of the flesh. They carry its scars yet. they will bear them upon them to their grave. And they can tell, alas! what a defeat cost them in that strife, what a cold cutting knife at the very heart, what self-accusation, self-abhorrence, self-despair, what an abject, shameful, ignominious return—the shield lost, the banner left behind—to *the Captain of their salvation*[1]*!* And therefore these can understand what sin has to do with suffering, and how he who fights with his sins in Christ's name may well be called a partaker in Christ's sufferings. As He *resisted unto blood, striving against sin*[2], so also must we. It is a life and death battle for each one of us. We shall never have done with it, for long together, while life lasts. Sometimes by craft, and sometimes by assault, sometimes by ambush, sometimes by feigned flight, sometimes with parade of arms and trumpets as though secure of intimidation and of triumph, the old enemy attacks again, the old sin rises from its fall, and there is nothing before us, yet once more, save hard-earned victory or shameful defeat.

In the midst of all, let this word be your stay: *Greater is He that is in you, than he that is in the world*[3].

Behold, an host compassed the city both with horses and chariots And the servant of Elisha said unto him, Alas, my master! how shall we do? And he answered, Fear not: for they that be with us are more than they that be with them. And Elisha prayed, and said, Lord, I pray Thee, open his eyes, that he may see.

---

[1] Heb. ii. 10.   [2] Heb. xii. 4   [3] 1 Joh iv. 4.

And the Lord opened the eyes of the young man, and he saw; and behold, the mountain was full of horses and chariots of fire round about Elisha[1].

It is a true parable. Thus it is still, for all who truly desire to know Christ—to know the power of His resurrection—to know the fellowship of His sufferings.

[1] 2 Kings vi 15—17.

SECOND SUNDAY IN LENT,
March 16, 1862.

LECTURE XVI.

PHILIPPIANS III. 12—16.

12 *Not that I already received, or am already perfected · but I am pressing on, if I may even grasp that thing with a*
13 *view to which I was also grasped by Christ. Brethren, I*[1] *do not reckon myself*[1] *to have grasped: but one thing—forgetting the things behind, and straining to the uttermost after the*
14 *things before, I press on, according to the mark, to the prize*
15 *of the high calling of God in Christ Jesus. Let us then, as many as are perfect, be thus minded. And if in anything ye are otherwise minded, even this shall God reveal to you.*
16 *Only—a thing which we* [have] *reached—walk by the same rule, be of the same mind*[2].

---

[1] In the original language there is a stress upon these pronouns.

[2] If, as in some editions, the words *rule*, &c. (to the end) be omitted, the sense will become, *Only, whatever thing we* [have] *reached, by the same thing walk;* that is, *let whatever attainments you have made in knowledge and grace be the rule and standard of your conduct.*

LECTURE XVI.

PHILIPPIANS III. 13.

Forgetting those things which are behind, and reaching forth unto those things which are before.

So strong had been the emphasis with which St Paul stated his hopes and aims in becoming a Christian—the gaining Christ, and being found in Him—the knowing Christ, and the power of His resurrection, and the fellowship of His sufferings— the being conformed to His death, if thus he might attain to His resurrection—that it might almost seem as if he represented the whole work as done, the victory already gained, the goal actually reached. It might have been said, This man considers himself to be no longer as other men are: he exhibits himself to us as a specimen and model of absolute perfection. And the profession of perfection is as evil in its effects as it is false in fact. It is a delusion in itself, and it acts as a discouragement to others. To disclaim such an assumption; to state explicitly what he is not, as well as what he is; to shew what a Christian may say of himself, and what he cannot say, consistently with true humility; is the object of the paragraph which comes before us to-day.

Not that I already received, or am already perfected[1]. Do not suppose me to mean that, when I became a Christian, I at once received, or that I have even now received, the whole thing aimed at and proposed to me. The word rendered *attained* in the 12th verse is a different word from that rendered *attain* in the 11th. And some confusion is introduced by the use of the same term in our English Version in the two places. St Paul is not correcting the idea that he had already *attained to the resurrection of the dead*, but that he had already *received* the thing for which he was seeking, whether fulness of knowledge, fulness of experience, or fulness of happiness. He is still seeking, though he is ever finding too.

But I am pressing on, if I may even grasp that thing with a view to which I was also grasped by Christ. He represents himself as having been seized, arrested, laid hold upon, by Christ Himself. No word could be more forcible, or more appropriate to that sudden interposition of our Lord Himself which turned an enemy and a blasphemer into a humble and devoted Christian. *I was grasped by Christ.*

[1] *Verse* 12.

But this seizure of him by Christ had an object. It was with a view to something. And that was, that St Paul, in his turn, might seize, might grasp, might lay hold upon, a certain possession. And that possession was of the nature of a prize. It was set before him as the result of exertion ; of an exertion like that of one who runs a long and arduous race against a number of formidable competitors. That is the figure. *I am pressing on*, says the Christian runner, *in the hope that I may even grasp that prize, with a view to which*, that I might thus gain it, *I was also grasped*, seized upon, arrested, apprehended, and thus set in the way towards it, *by Christ* Himself.

Brethren, I do not reckon myself to have grasped[1] this prize. Whatever others may think of me, or whatever others may think of themselves, that is not my estimate of my position. I regard myself as still engaged in the contest, not as already possessed of the prize.

But one thing—this, and this only, is what I allow myself to do—*forgetting the things behind*, leaving behind my back that part of the course which I have already traversed, *and straining to the uttermost after the things before*, stretching every muscle to get over that part of the course which has still to be accomplished, *I press on, according to the mark*, guided solely by the object which indicates to the eye the

[1] *Verse* 13

end of the course, *to the prize*, there to be received, at the mark or goal, *of the high calling of God in Christ Jesus*[1]. I am ever speeding on towards that goal at which I shall receive the prize to which God invited me, when in the person of Christ Jesus He called to me from heaven. The *high calling* here is the *heavenly calling* of the third chapter of the Epistle to the Hebrews; where all Christians are addressed as *holy brethren, partakers of a heavenly calling*[2]. God in heaven calls to us, and offers us a rest in heaven.

Let us then, as many as are perfect, all we who are no longer babes, but of mature age, in the Christian life, *be thus minded*[3]. *I have transferred these things in a figure to myself*[4]*:* but they are meant for all. It is not I only who am called to a glory and a blessedness which makes me count all things else but dross and damage in comparison with it. And it is not I only who feel the necessity of remembering that I am still a candidate, still a runner; not yet possessed of the prize, but speeding towards it. These things belong to all: this ought to be the mind of all those who would not forfeit their birthright as men in Christ. In particular, it is one sign of Christian perfection—in the only sense in which that word can be applied to the life that is—to be conscious of imperfection. *Not that I am already*

[1] *Verse* 14. [2] Heb. iii. 1. [3] *Verse* 15. [4] 1 Cor. iv. 6.

perfected should be the heart's language of all *as many as be perfect.*

And if in anything ye are otherwise minded, even this shall God reveal to you. If in any respect you who are Christians in sincerity are at present even in mistake and error, the God whom you serve will in due time dispel that error, and supply that which is lacking in your knowledge. A comforting thought, my brethren, for all those who feel that they are indeed seeking God, and serving Him according to the measure of the light they have! If there be any point on which at present your knowledge or feeling is at fault, rest assured that God will not suffer you to remain in error, but will gradually complete your knowledge, and gradually correct your feeling, till He brings you into the light of perfect day

Only, at all events (for this is *a thing which we* have *reached*) *walk by the same rule, be of the same mind*[1]. In many respects, individual attainments will vary: but there is one thing to which we have all attained; there is one direction not beyond the attainment of any of us; and that is, unity of rule, and unity of feeling. If you cannot as yet all see all things alike, at least you can all recognize the same Divine Word and the same Divine Spirit as the rule of opinion and the guide of conduct, and you can all manifest that unity of principle by a life of love.

[1] *Verse* 16.

And thus St Paul returns, once again, to the inculcation of that Christian unity which seems to have been the one subject of his anxiety in reference to the Philippian Church. Would that the same voice might be heard also in our own! If you cannot all see things with the same eyes, at least you may agree to differ, and at least you may walk in love.

The general sense of these five verses may be expressed thus.

I have spoken of high aims and glorious hopes. Do not misunderstand me. I am not saying that desire and attainment are in me as yet one. I have given up all that I had, and I have trampled under foot all that I was, for the sake of gaining Christ, of knowing Christ. I want to feel in myself the power of His resurrection I want to be perfectly conformed to His death; to be in every point a partaker of His sufferings. And thus I hope to reach at last the blessed resurrection; man's one hope, the Church's one expectation. But in all this I am still a struggling, not a resting man. When Christ called to me from heaven, it was to tell me of a glorious prize: when He laid His hand upon me from heaven, it was to point out to me a course and a goal; it was to set my feet stedfastly in that course, and to fix my view resolutely upon that goal. He never deceived me, nor do I deceive myself, with the hope of an easy race or of a swift arrival[1]. *I know that I am*

---

[1] *Verse 12.*

still running and to run. What then? I accept the condition[1]. *I stay not to look behind me; to congratulate myself upon difficulties surmounted or competitors outstripped. My business lies, not with the course behind, but with the course before me. Every power of joint and limb must be put forth to the uttermost: there is no resting in that race: to relax is to stop, to stop is to go backward. I still hear in my ear the heavenly call: I still have in my eye the mark which is the goal. Onward, onward, onward still: while this life lasts, till that life opens, the Christian must walk and not be weary, he must run and not faint*[2]. *Be this your mind, Christian brethren, if you would be perfect! Lesser differences there may be, there will be, among you: points of doubt, yea, points of error: for God is patient and merciful, and what you know not now He will shew hereafter*[3]. *But one thing you can all do; one attainment you have all reached: you can all seek truth at the same fountain, and you can all forgive as you have been all forgiven*[4].

My brethren, I would propose to you this morning the example of St Paul as it is here set before us by himself. *Be ye followers of me, as I also am of Christ*[5]. *Forgetting those things which are behind, and reaching forth unto those things which are before.* Can a Christian minister, and particularly at a season dedicated by the Church to purposes of self-examination

[1] *Verse* 13. [2] *Verse* 14. [3] *Verse* 15.
[4] *Verse* 16. [5] 1 Cor. xi 1.

and repentance, counsel his congregation to forget the past? A few plain words in answer to that question will form the best application of the words read to you as the text.

1. i The past has its uses. Not for nothing did God bestow upon us memory. Not for nothing do His servants recollect themselves, look back, call to mind, remember. We want the past, all of us, for purposes of humiliation. What a process, in each one, is that of taking down pride! What a process! how long, how tedious, how often to be begun again! We can scarcely bear a word of praise, or a thought of self-congratulation, the best of us. How pleasant it is, for the moment, to have self flattered, caressed, humoured! How tranquil does it make us for the moment, how conciliatory, how agreeable! And then it stings like a viper It upsets the balance of the spirit, and we soon make ourselves, under its influence, ridiculous and contemptible. We cannot bear praise: it soon runs into self-complacency: and what a state is that for a struggling man, and for a sinner!

Now in the great work of humbling pride memory has a most important office. We might almost content ourselves, if we desired to destroy the self-conceit of any member of this present congregation, with saying to him, Let memory work: think of that shameful fall which you had yesterday or the day before; that broken resolution, that outbreak of temper, that irreverent worship, that omitted duty, that secret sin thought of if not done. Yes, my brethren, I scarcely see how he can be proud whose memory is not dormant. We must not entirely *forget the things behind*, so far as our past sins are concerned, if we would be humble as we ought to be.

ii. Again, we want the past for purposes of admonition and warning It is thence that we draw experience. A man cannot live out half his days without becoming wise as to his failings and his infirmities. If we were in such sense new men every morning as that the past were a blank and the future a conjecture, we should be far worse equipped than we are for the work and for the conflict of the present. It is because we have had experience of ourselves, because we have found out by painful trial what snares are most insidious to us and what assaults most formidable, that we can shape our onward course, if we be true to ourselves, with something of foresight and discretion, anticipating and forecasting, forewarned and forearmed, looking before because looking after.

2. But there are two senses in which we ought all of us to forget the things behind.

i. It is possible that upon some the remembrance of the past may have an elating influence. It is possible, I say, though indeed it is hard to believe it. We have read of persons, in biographies and in history, who were tempted to rely upon the past for salvation. Persons who have even said, Safe once, safe for ever: I am sure I was safe once, and therefore I am sure that I am safe for ever. That perhaps is not a very common form of error: but not without reason do I say here, that there are those who trust too much to a past conversion and look too little to a present consistency. There are those, alas! whose whole religious history, read in the light of truth, would be this, Conversion, without change: one season of excitement, a paroxysm of repentance, followed by an ecstasy of faith; and then a life of resting upon the oars, of relying upon grace once given, of remembering light and of walking on in darkness. May we not urge upon such persons, if such indeed there should be now amongst us, the example, here before us, of the blessed Apostle St Paul? Might he not have said, in a sense above that possible for other men, *Have I not seen Jesus Christ our Lord*[1], and can I therefore doubt that I am one of His called and chosen? Hear him then disclaiming utterly any such trust; telling how he forgets the things behind, and reaches forth only to the things before; nay, declaring his conviction, in express terms, that he might even *have preached to others*, and yet himself *be a castaway*[2]!

    ii. It is possible, I say, that upon some persons

[1] 1 Cor. ix. 1.   [2] 1 Cor. ix. 27

the past may have an elating influence; and it is certain that where this is so, there is, most of all, need of the warning to forget the things behind. But far commoner is the opposite risk: far more in number are they whom the thought of the past deeply depresses. How many are there, especially among the young—while conscience is still tender, and the *terrors* of God are *suffered with a troubled mind*[1]— upon whom the experience of the past acts with a paralyzing influence! They view with suspicion every conscious working of good within, because they have so often, in former cases, found such impulses ineffectual. They no longer hope anything from a softening of the heart, such as is sometimes vouchsafed to us, towards God our Father, towards Christ our Saviour, because they have so often before found it a transitory and an ineffective influence. They fold their hands in the presence of temptation; they lose all courage and all spirit for resistance; they summon to their aid, at such moments, neither a resolute will nor the surer and mightier aid of God's holy and promised Spirit; because they have so often before found the tempter too strong for them, and because they will look back instead of looking onwards. May it not well be said to such persons, *Forget the things behind?* If you are growing proud, look back for a moment upon your errors and falls,

[1] Psalm lxxxviii. 15. P. B.

upon your backslidings and sins, that you may be corrected and humbled: if you are growing careless, fancying your course open and your success secure, look back for more than a moment upon the history of perils past, of unsuspected but most real snares, of circumstances apparently harmless but found to be full of danger to the soul, that you may be warned by that experience to walk more warily and more closely with your God. But when the question is of courage or of cowardice, of resistance or of flight, then forget the things behind; let past falls be forgotten, let past proofs of weakness be disregarded and dismissed; put your trust in God, and in His name and in His strength go forward!

If only we will keep the two parts of the text combined, we need not qualify the use of either. *Forget the things behind*, if it stood by itself, might be a dangerous maxim: obeying it, we might become proud, we might become trifling, we might become presumptuous. Add to it, *and reach forth to the things before*, and it can be only salutary, only saving. It is not rest to which we are called: human indolence is ever asking for it, human impatience, if it come not, will seize it at all risks. But we must not seek to hasten what God has postponed: we must not ask to close our journey at noonday, or to reach the goal before the course is traversed. It is one of the highest objects of these our weekly gatherings, to rouse one another, by prayer and by the ministry of the Word[1], to greater diligence and greater watchfulness, to a higher hope and to a more sustained exertion. And indeed there is much that we can do for one another in this matter. Everything that one can tell of comfort given, of strength vouchsafed, of a Saviour's grace communicated to him, is a positive help to another in arousing his flagging energies and quickening his languid steps. God grant that this occasion may have been the means, in His hand, of doing this for some of His people! Does not the text itself say to us, Your business is with the present and with the future; *let the dead past bury its dead*[2]? Dwell not in the charnel-house of disappointed hopes and frustrated endeavours. Grope not in the darkness of departed joys, or of ill-aimed and abortive efforts, or of wasted and neglected opportunities. Not there, not there, lies either duty, strength, or benefit. The past is past, and cannot now be altered or undone. It is gone in to its account; take heed lest the present, which is slipping away each moment, follow it with as sad a record! God calls to you from heaven—calls still, though long disregarded: He bids you enter His course, He bids you hasten towards His goal. He promises that the past shall be forgiven you, if even now, even thus late, you will begin to *run with patience the race set before us*[3]. *To them that have no*

[1] Acts vi 4.   [2] Luke ix. 60.   [3] Heb. xii. 1.

might He increaseth strength[1]*:* He *worketh in us both to will and to do of His good pleasure*[2]. Go ye also[3] into the course, and *so run that ye may obtain*[4] *!* God give us grace to incite one another to greater earnestness in running that race in which if there is room for emulation, there is none for envying; in which, rather, the success of one is the happiness of another; in which there is a crown for every faithful runner, a separate welcome hereafter from His lips whom (though unseen) each had loved[5], and in whose unclouded presence all shall rest together for ever!

[1] Isai. xl. 29.   [2] Phil. ii. 13.   [3] Matt. xx. 7.
[4] 1 Cor. ix. 24.   [5] 1 Pet. i. 8

THIRD SUNDAY IN LENT,
March 23, 1862.

LECTURE XVII.

PHILIPPIANS III. 17—21.

17 BECOME my fellow-imitators, brethren; and mark those
18 who so walk even as ye have a pattern [in] us. For many
walk, of whom I often spoke to you, and now speak even
19 weeping, [as] the enemies of the cross of Christ, whose end
is destruction, whose god is their appetite, and [whose] glory
is in their shame, whose mind is upon things on the earth.
20 For our citizenship is already in heaven, whence we are
21 expecting also a Saviour, the Lord Jesus Christ, who
shall transfigure the body of our abasement [so as to be] of
one form with the body of His glory, by (according to) the
operation of His power even to subject to Him all things.

LECTURE XVII.

PHILIPPIANS III 19, 20.

Who mind earthly things...For our conversation is in heaven.

ST PAUL was a very real man. He spoke naturally, he spoke truthfully, and he spoke plainly. He called things by their true names, and he designated men, whether himself or others, by their true character. We shall notice in the passage now to be read two illustrations of this remark. In him there is no false modesty, and there is no false charity. All is simple, and all is true.

The last five verses of the chapter are our subject to-day. If God by His Holy Spirit be with us in pondering them, we shall find them full of instruction and full of admonition.

Brethren, so the 17th verse opens, *be followers together of me*. The expression is, more exactly, *Become imitators together, fellow-imitators, of me, brethren*. This word *imitators* is peculiar (with a single exception[1]) to St Paul's writings, if we may include among them for the moment the Epistle to the Hebrews. *Be ye imitators of me,* he writes to the Corinthians, *even as I also am of Christ*[2]. *Ye became imitators,* so he writes to the Thessalonians, *of us and of the Lord*[3] *Be ye,* he says to the Ephesians, *imitators of God, as dear children*[4] The compound word *fellow-imitators* occurs only in the verse now before us. And we must feel it to be a remarkable expression It is remarkable that so humble a person as St Paul should propose himself to the churches as an example. If we had not abundant proofs of the accuracy of his self-knowledge and of the sincerity of his self-abasement, we might almost think that the charge to imitate him bordered upon presumption, upon self-righteousness. As it is— that supposition being excluded by what we know of him as a man, and as an inspired man, from other evidence—I draw from it rather this inference · What an entire self-devotion, and what a perfect integrity of mind and life, must there have been in him, to account for so humble a person using language so emphatic concerning himself! I suppose there is no one in this congregation who would so speak of himself even to his own children; no one who would

---

[1] 1 Pet iii. 13. [2] 1 Cor. xi. 1. [3] 1 Thess. i. 6.
[4] Eph. v. 1.

dare to propose himself as a model or an example, in all respects, to those most closely connected with him. Do we rejoice in that inability as a sign of good? No doubt, it is better than false pretension or spiritual pride. but would it not be well if there were more amongst us, who could say firmly and with a good conscience, Notwithstanding many faults and many infirmities, I can yet appeal to the Searcher of hearts as to the integrity of my purpose and as to the completeness of my self-surrender; I can say, so far as purity of motive and transparency of conscience is concerned, Imitate me, and mark those who walk as ye have me for your example? There is quite as often a spirit of indolence and a spirit of self-complacency, as of genuine and profound humility, in that language of self-disparagement and self-abasement of which the religious world in our times judges so favourably.

Be ye, St Paul writes, *become ye*, or *prove yourselves, my fellow-imitators, brethren:* set yourselves with one mind to imitate me: *and mark*, for approval and for companionship, *those who so walk*, so conduct themselves, *even as ye have a pattern*, or *model*, in *us*[1]. The words are very strong. To use them, a man must have been either a great self-deceiver or a very devoted Christian. We know which St Paul was. O that there were more like him amongst ourselves!

[1] *Verse* 17.

He goes on to say that there is room for the caution, both as regards the following and the setting of such an example.

For many walk, of whom I often spoke to you, and now speak even weeping, as *the enemies of the cross of Christ*[1]*; whose end is destruction, whose god is their appetite, and* whose *glory is in their shame, whose mind is upon things on the earth*[2]. The conduct of many is that which I often described to you when I was with you. I told you then, and I tell you now, the tears falling as I write, that there are those, and that they are many, who can only be described as *enemies of the cross of Christ:* whatever they may profess, however much they may speak of faith in the Gospel, their true name is that of foes of the cross: they are destined to a terrible end when Christ returns to judgment. their real idol is their own appetite; their real motive in professing the Gospel is the gain they can make of it: if they can avoid reproach, if they can please men, if they can *live of the Gospel*[3] as popular preachers or conspicuous partisans, *they have their reward*[4]*:* they know no higher motive than that which is altogether of the earth. And therefore I call them enemies of the cross. Its humbling, softening, transforming power, they know not, and they care not to know: its unselfishness,

---

[1] *Verse* 18.   [2] *Verse* 19.   [3] 1 Cor. ix. 14
[4] Matt. vi. 5

its unworldliness, its holiness, its mortification of the flesh, its substitution of the future for the present, of the unseen for the visible, of heaven for earth, is a mere riddle or a mere offence to them: they belong to this life, where their heart and their affection and their treasure is.

How opposite is this, he says, to the life to which I call you!

For our citizenship is already in heaven; whence we are expecting also a Saviour, the Lord Jesus Christ[1]. Others have their mind set upon things below: appetite is their god: they make the Gospel itself a means of worldly gain· what they pride themselves upon is just what a Christian should be ashamed of. and *the end of these things is death*[2]; when the world perishes, its children and its subjects must perish too. But we are not of the world Already, even in this life, *our citizenship is in heaven;* and thither is our eye ever turned, in expectation of His coming, who is even now our King, and shall one day be our Deliverer and our Saviour too.

And is He not our Saviour now? He is. Already the dead soul has felt His quickening power, and has passed, by the very act of faith, from death unto life. Already day by day it is renewed by God's Holy Spirit: *He wakeneth, morning by morning, mine ear to hear*[3] and my heart to feel. There is a sense there-

[1] *Verse* 20.   [2] Rom. vi. 21.   [3] Isai. l. 4.

fore in which deliverance, redemption, salvation, are of the past and of the present: *we are saved*[1], and *we are being saved*[2]: but there is a sense too in which we are still *looking for a Saviour*. *Ourselves also*, St Paul writes to the Romans, *though we have the firstfruits of the Spirit, even we ourselves groan in ourselves, waiting for an adoption, even the redemption of our body*[3]. This redemption of the dead body, to be the handmaid and the habitation, through eternal ages, of the already redeemed soul, is described to us in the words which remain.

Who shall transfigure the body of our abasement so as to be *of one form with the body of His glory, by (according to) the operation of His power even to subject to Him all things*[4]. That is St Paul's account of the resurrection (or equivalent transformation) of the body. *We shall not all sleep*, he says to the Corinthians, *but we shall all be changed*[5]: we shall not all undergo the process of death; there will be a generation alive upon the earth when the Saviour comes; but even they, though they die not, must be changed. *this corruptible must put on (clothe itself with) incorruption, and this mortal must put on immortality*[6]. *flesh and blood cannot inherit the kingdom of God, neither doth corruption inherit incorruption*[7]. This body, as it

[1] Eph ii 5.
[2] 1 Cor. xv 2.
[3] Rom viii 23.
[4] *Verse* 21.
[5] 1 Cor xv 51
[6] 1 Cor. xv 53
[7] 1 Cor xv 50.

now is, could not exist in heaven. It must be dissolved, decomposed, and reconstructed. At present, it is a *body of abasement* or humiliation: a constant memento of the fall, a constant clog upon the regenerated soul, a constant inlet of temptation, a constant lurking-place and lodging-house of sin. What is to be done with it? Is it enough that it should be put off, laid aside, suffered to decay, and never resumed? Is it enough that the soul should make its escape, flee away to a land of shadows, and be at rest? Philosophers answered, Yes; that is what we hope, that is what we long for, that is what we guess at as the perfection of the wise, as the consummation of the virtuous. St Paul answers, No: a disembodied soul is but half a man; enough perhaps for rest, but not enough for action; suited to an intermediate state of refreshment and repose from labour; not suited to an eternal state, in which men shall be *equal to the angels*[1], not more in the vision of God than in the excellence of their strength and in the performance of His beneficent will[2].

When the Saviour comes again, for whom it is the business of a Christian's life to be ever waiting and watching, He will come to transfigure the body of our earthly humiliation into the form of His own body of glory. We know not indeed, and in this life we cannot know, what that change is: the conception of

[1] Luke xx. 36.   [2] Ps. ciii. 20.

spirit is beyond our capacity, much more the conception of a spiritual body[1]. But there are ideas, and there are revelations too, which we must accept and ponder and cherish, though we cannot fathom and can scarcely grasp; and this is one of them: not death, but resurrection, is the Christian's consummation; not the disjunction, but the reunion, of soul and body; a reunion of the soul that departed to the body that died, in such sort that the identity shall be certain, though the change be immense[2].

Nor are these ideas, these revelations, mere words, mere sounds, to us, even now. The pattern of the human body in its resurrection shall be the body of our Lord Jesus Christ as already raised. In His Transfiguration He gave to the chosen three a glimpse of that coming glory they saw Him marvellously transformed, *the fashion of His countenance altered*[3], the humble human figure elevated and illuminated; their eyes were dazzled with the brightness of that light, and yet they saw beyond all question that their Master, and none else, was before them. In that memorable event the resurrection was foreshadowed; the resurrection of *Christ the firstfruits*, the resurrection of *them that are Christ's at His coming*[4]. Well might St Peter dwell, in the later years of life, upon the confirmation of the faith

---

[1] 1 Cor. xv. 44. [2] 2 Cor. v 1—4. [3] Luke ix. 29.
[4] 1 Cor. xv. 23.

there afforded. Well may he say in his second Epistle, knowing that he must shortly put off his tabernacle, *We have also*, in the revelations of *the holy mount* of transfiguration, *the prophetic word* made *more sure*[1], more firm and certain to the foot that would rest upon it. They who had seen the Saviour assume for a moment upon earth His body of glory, and had heard from heaven the accompanying voice, *This is my beloved Son, in whom I am well pleased*[2], could better understand how it might be that the permanent assumption of that form should be consistent with the identity of the Person, how it might be also that *the hope of Israel*[3] and the hope of mankind should one day be realized in the resurrection of the body.

And when at last the same disciples and their brethren saw the risen Saviour as He appeared to them during the forty days between resurrection and ascension[4]; when they noticed how He had become independent of the accidents and circumstances of the body, bound no longer by laws of space and motion[5], by necessities of food and rest, by limitations of sight and sense, and yet how entirely the Saviour who rose was in every point the Saviour who died[6]; when they were taught thus by experience how unessential to thought and action are the conditions of bodily life

[1] 2 Pet. 1. 18, 19 [2] Matt. xvii. 5. [3] Acts xxviii. 20.
[4] 1 Cor. xv. 5—7. [5] John xx. 19. [6] Luke xxiv. 39

below, how they may all drop off from us and yet leave us the same, only freer, more vigorous, and more powerful, than before; did they not learn that lesson, which for us is so difficult, of the difference between a disembodied soul and a risen man? did they not begin to understand why even the repose of the blessed dead should be spoken of as a poor thing in comparison with the redemption of the body, why it should be made the very keystone of the Gospel arch that God will raise the dead, that Christ at His coming will transfigure our body of humiliation into the form of His body of glory by the operation of His resistless power to subdue all things to Himself?

These closing words will give energy to the thought which I have reserved as the application of the whole; the contrast here exhibited between the man who minds earthly things, and the Christian whose citizenship is already in heaven.

There is a force in the original expression which has scarcely yet been drawn out to you. It is, *who have earthly things for their sentiment*, for their thought and for their feeling. And this state is opposed to that of him who lives upon earth as a citizen of heaven.

If anything for a moment shews us to ourselves as we are, stripping off the disguise by which we commonly impose not upon others only but upon our own selves, does anything strike us so painfully as this one conviction, that we are predominantly earthly-minded? that, whatever else we may be or not be, we have *things on the earth* for our thought and for our feeling? Suppose some terrible calamity befalls us, making havoc of our prospects below; one of those events—and they are many—which make it impossible that we should ever rise higher in life than we are at this moment, that we should ever be richer or more distinguished or more powerful than now: suppose yet a little more, that something has occurred not only to forbid our rising higher but involving as its sure consequence our even sinking lower, something which must take away from our present consideration, our present advantages, or our present comforts; has any one here known and felt such a blow? or can any one place himself in thought under this infliction? Will he tell me what he really has left to him when earth is thus darkened, thus impoverished? Do his hopes and his affections rise instantly, rise naturally, rise instinctively, to his home above? Is he able at once to say, not only, *Thy will, O God, be done*[1], but also, *It is well*[2], my chief treasure is not touched; it lies out of reach, and my heart with it[3]? It is easy in days of prosperity to take it for granted that earth is not all to us, that of course we have heaven too, and that of course we care a thousand-fold more for it than for the other: it is not while earth is ours that we feel ourselves to be most addicted to it: it is when earth is taken away

[1] Matt vi 10. [2] 2 Kings iv. 26. [3] Matt. vi. 21.

that we find to our dismay, too often, that our heaven is gone also! There is a quietude and a self-complacency in worldly success, which puts us as it were in good humour with both worlds, with God above and man below. But take one world away, and what has become of the other? It is a mistake to suppose that affliction, in any form, drives men to God. It may in time, with pains and prayer and many struggles, make the heavenly-minded man more heavenly-minded: but it might almost be said of it that it has an opposite effect upon the godless and the earthly-minded, at once shewing him his state and fixing that state upon him. *He that is unjust, let him be unjust still · and he that is holy, let him be holy still*[1].

Look well, my brethren—let us all do so—into the condition of our heart's affections. Have we any real interest in things above? Do we know what it is to read the Bible, not as a duty, but as a pleasure, as containing an account of a *land very far off*[2] yet much desired; of a Person *whom not having seen we love*[3]*?* Does it ever cross our minds to wish the journey ended and the heavenly home reached? and this not from mere weariness, and not from impatience of discipline, and not from faint-heartedness or mistrust of God, but from a real desire to be altogether holy, in God's presence, like Christ, and seeing Him as He is? It is rather by positives than by negatives that we ascertain

[1] Rev. xxii. 11.   [2] Isai. xxxiii. 17.   [3] 1 Pet. i. 8.

our true condition. There are those who make it the one test of a person's fitness to die, whether he was resigned, whether he could give up his children, whether he could say that he had no wish to live. A poor, feeble, miserable criterion! Ask rather, Did he shew an interest in things above? Was there any sign not only of his having done with earth, but of his having found heaven? Did he shew that his affections were there? Did he speak and feel as a citizen of the better country? Had he regarded the laws of that land? had he loved its subjects? had he been loyal to its King? Had he felt towards it as an Englishman abroad feels towards England, counting the days till his eyes shall once more see its white cliffs and his feet tread once more its green pastures? These things, if we know them not for another, we can know for ourselves: and depend upon it, he, and he only, who has a country above will ever sit loose to interests below: if we would ever escape the terrible condemnation of having minded earthly things, it must be because God, of His infinite mercy, in answer to earnest prayer, and for the sake alone of our most blessed Saviour, has given us the comfort and joy of being able to say from the heart, My home is not here; my *citizenship is in heaven!*

FOURTH SUNDAY IN LENT,
March 30, 1862.

LECTURE XVIII.

PHILIPPIANS IV. 1—7.

1 *T*HEREFORE, my brethren beloved and longed after, my joy
2 and crown, so stand fast in the Lord, beloved. I beseech
Euodia, and I beseech Syntyche, to be of the same mind in
3 the Lord. Yea, I entreat thee also, genuine yokefellow, help
them; for they struggled together with me in the Gospel,
with Clemens also and my other fellow-workers, whose names
4 are in a book of life. Rejoice in the Lord always; again I
5 will say it, Rejoice Let your gentleness be known unto all
6 men. The Lord is near. Be anxious about nothing, but in
every thing by prayer and supplication with thanksgiving
7 let your requests be made known before God. And the peace
of God, which surpasses every understanding, shall guard
your hearts and your thoughts in Christ Jesus.

LECTURE XVIII.

PHILIPPIANS IV. 5, 6.

The Lord is at hand. Be careful for nothing

WE enter to-day upon the last chapter of the Epistle which has occupied us for some months. We have heard, in many particulars, what St Paul's view of the Christian's life was. *To me to live is Christ*[1]. *Let this mind be in you, which was also in Christ Jesus. Work out your own salvation with fear and trembling; for it is God which worketh in you*[2]. *That I may win Christ, and be found in Him. That I may know Him, and the power of His resurrection, and the fellowship of His sufferings. Forgetting the things behind, and reaching forth unto the things before, I press toward the mark*[3]. He has called upon them to follow (imitate) him; and to remember that there are two ways of living, even within the professed Church of

---

[1] Phil. 1. 21.   [2] Chap. 11. 5, 12.
[3] Chap. 111. 8, 9, 10, 13.

Christ[1]. There are those *who mind earthly things*, and there are those whose *citizenship is already in heaven*[2]. Hence the need of perpetual care, watchfulness, and godly fear.

Therefore, my brethren beloved and longed after, my joy and crown, so stand fast in the Lord, beloved[3].

These being the dangers and these the hopes of a Christian, be stedfast; not deserters, not waverers, not triflers, not loiterers, but resolute, earnest, vigorous men; that I may number you in the day of Christ amongst those faithful disciples who shall be the joy and the crown of my ministry and of my apostleship. That it may be so, remember your one safeguard: *stand fast*, not in yourselves, but *in the Lord;* not in your own good resolutions, endeavours, or past successes, but in the living grace of Him who has all power in heaven and in earth[4].

I beseech Euodia, and I beseech Syntyche, to be of the same mind in the Lord[5].

Two Christian women at Philippi—yes, Christian women still—were unhappily at variance. They must be reconciled. Let the entreaty of their beloved Apostle, powerful, no doubt, in the heart of each separately, be the means of reuniting them *in the Lord*. Let there be no schism in the one body[6]. Are there any two Christian women in this congregation, divided,

---

[1] Chap. iii 17, 18, 19. [2] Chap. iii 20. [3] *Verse* 1.
[4] Matt xxviii 18. [5] *Verse* 2 [6] 1 Cor. xii 25

unhappily, in feeling and friendship, by some one of those infinite differences which beset our infirm condition in this life? Let them come together again in their common Lord! Let this holy season, telling of His earthly struggles and sufferings for each, be the occasion of a reconciliation and reunion not again to be broken for ever!

Yea, I intreat thee also, my *genuine yokefellow*[1]. We know not who is addressed. Some one at Philippi whom St Paul designates as his own sincere and genuine comrade in the toils and struggles of the ministry. *Help them.* aid the two Christian women mentioned above, in the sometimes difficult work of reconciliation; bring them together, be a peacemaker between them; *for they struggle together with me,* they joined in my conflict or contest, *in the Gospel,* in the work of recommending and spreading the Gospel, *with Clemens also and my other fellow-workers, whose names are in a book of life.*

There is a work for women as well as for men in the Church of Christ. A woman may labour with an Apostle in the Gospel. Without departing one step from the propriety of her position or the delicacy of her character, she can *work a good work*[2] for Christ, and for the performance or neglect of it she must hereafter give account. By example, by influence, by meek endurance, by active sympathy,

[1] *Verse 3.* [2] Matt. xxvi. 10.

she can do that which a man cannot do, in the society of her equals and in the homes of the suffering.

The names of those who are sincerely serving Christ on earth are already *in a book of life. Notwithstanding in this rejoice not,* our Lord said on the triumphant return of the seventy disciples, *that the spirits are subject unto you; but rather rejoice, because your names are written in heaven*[1]. That book is already in existence: already it is full of names: hereafter it shall be opened. *And whosoever was not found written in the book of life was cast into the lake of fire*[2].

Rejoice in the Lord always: again I will say it, Rejoice[3].

He speaks as if it were in a Christian's power to do the thing which he says. He speaks as if joy, perpetual joy, were not more a gift than a grace; not more a blessing than a duty. Some of us not only suffer from depression, but cherish it. There is a pathos about it, which they sometimes mistake for piety. Let them listen to the charge here addressed to all Christians: *Rejoice in the Lord; rejoice always; I will say it yet again, Rejoice.* To rejoice is in one sense a happiness, in another sense it is a duty. In one aspect, it is an art; there are those who contrive to rejoice, find food for joy, where others can see nothing but gloom and grief.

[1] Luke x. 20. [2] Rev. xx. 15 [3] *Verse* 4.

in another aspect, it is an attainment; a result arrived at by long experience, in the later days of a consistent Christian course   But in every point of view, Christian joy can be found only *in the Lord*[1]; by communion with Him, by close watching, by living much in things above. Compromises with the world drive it away. Sin destroys it in a moment.

Let your gentleness be known unto all men[2]. Let all those with whom you have any intercourse find you gentle, forbearing, kind ; in particular, let them find you willing to relax and forego your strict rights, not punctilious about trifles, examples of that charity which *seeketh not her own, is not provoked,* and *reckoneth not the evil ;* which *beareth all things, believeth all things, hopeth all things, endureth all things*[3].

The Lord is near. Soon He will come again, to receive you for ever to Himself[4]. Already the *Judge standeth before the door*[5]. Already too, and always, He is near in another sense. He is ever at hand to hear and to answer prayer. Therefore *be anxious about nothing; but in everything by prayer and supplication with thanksgiving let your requests be made known before God*[6]. *And the peace of God, which surpasses every understanding*—which in its fulness is beyond the reach of any human comprehension, nay, which in itself, in its very first beginnings,

[1] Ps. civ. 34. P. B.   [2] *Verse 5.*   [3] 1 Cor xiii. 5, 7.
[4] Joh. xiv. 3.   [5] James v. 9.   [6] *Verse 6.*

transcends the sphere of the subtlest of human intellects—*shall guard your hearts and your thoughts in Christ Jesus*[1].

The peace of God shall guard your hearts. It shall be the protection, yea, the keeper, of your hearts and of all their thoughts. The peace, the harmony of soul, the repose and concord of the whole man, which is God's gift, the effect of God's own presence by His Holy Spirit, shall keep you as in a fortified place from all danger, from all the crafts and from all the assaults of evil. What is it which exposes us to our worst perils? Is it not a roving heart? a heart seeking rest and finding none[2]? Is it not the unsatisfied, the insatiable thirst, which is in all of us by nature, for a happiness which yet earth cannot give? That is what makes a man a pleasure-hunter, that is what makes a man an idolater of the world, that is what makes a man the slave of his evil passions and sinful lusts. That is the bait which the devil presents to the fallen Adam: and if it succeeded even with the unfallen and the upright, who shall wonder if it succeeds with him? Let a man have found peace in God, let him have tasted of that water after drinking of which none thirsts again for any other[3], and he has a safeguard against evil. Why should he go after that which cannot profit, after that which cannot satisfy, when he has within him a very spring of living water?

[1] *Verse* 7. [2] Luke xi. 24. [3] Joh. iv. 14.

Now that is the sense in which St Paul writes that *the peace of God shall guard our hearts and our thoughts*, that is, the seat of thought, and the workings of thought. There will be no roving desires there to go abroad from the camp and fall into the enemy's ambush. And there will be no traitor there to open the gate of the citadel to some disguised foe. The heart that has found peace in God is kept, as in a sure fortress[1], by that very peace itself. It *is built as a city that is at unity in itself*[2]. It is all at one. It is not divided between this and that it is not, like the heart of nature, a fighting-ground of conflicting parties: it is in safe keeping under an almighty hand.

These thoughts will bring us back to the particular point selected for consideration to-day; the connection between the doctrine and the precept which form the text of this discourse; *The Lord is at hand: be careful for nothing*

It is not easy to determine in which of two senses the former clause is to be taken. *The Lord is near* in position; and *the Lord is near* in approach. In either sense we can connect the doctrine and the precept. If the Lord is soon coming, how idle must be all anxiety about things soon to be dissolved[3]! If the Lord is always present, how needless must be all anxiety about things easy of remedy! The two thoughts fall into one. But it is with the latter of

[1] Prov. xviii. 10. [2] Ps. cxxii. 3 P. B. [3] 2 Pet. iii. 11.

the two that I desire to occupy you now. The Lord Jesus Christ is always at hand; therefore turn all anxiety into prayer.

Thousands of hearts have found repose in this one word of inspiration. It is not a profitable speculation, which verse of the Bible has made the most converts or strengthened most disciples It is somewhat like the question with which Scribes and Pharisees of old perplexed themselves, *Master, which is the great commandment in the Law*[1]? But this we may say, that around particular verses of the Holy Word the minds and souls of Christ's servants have in all ages gathered as peculiarly bright and genial. And towards those special verses we cannot but feel as we do towards a place ennobled or consecrated by the footsteps of saints or heroes. Such verses have a history, as well as a doctrine: and is not this one of them?

The Lord is ever near; not more in the approach of His Advent, than in the reality of His spiritual presence *Wherever two or three are gathered together, there is He in the midst of them*[2]. Wherever, in perfect solitude or amidst the din of uncongenial sounds, one humble heart turns to Him as the Saviour and the Intercessor, there is He, not to be sought far and found late, but listening before speech, answering before entreaty[3]. Whatever we be, He

[1] Matt. xxii. 36.   [2] Matt. xviii. 20.   [3] Isai. lxv. 24.

changes not: if we doubt His presence, we disparage His power, we deny His divinity. Thus far, it is no question of our fitness : *the Lord is at hand*, be we good, or be we evil How ready, how just the inference, *Call ye upon Him while He is near*[1]*!*

But the nature of that calling upon Him, of that prayer to the present Saviour, will vary with the person To those who are either predominantly worldly, or else tied and bound with the chain of some definite sin, we would say, The Lord is still at hand, we know not for how long: call upon Him for illumination, call upon Him for conversion, call upon Him for deliverance, for healing, for mercy, for life! And to those who are wavering and undecided, not indifferent yet not awake, neither hot nor cold but lukewarm, we would say, The Lord is at hand, as truly as once on earth; thronged and pressed[2] by crowds of worshippers all calling Him *Lord, Lord*, but too little doing the things which He says[3]: now therefore come out from the multitude, and seek to touch Him; be not satisfied with that general, promiscuous, half-involuntary homage, but reach hither thy finger, and behold His pierced hands; reach hither thy hand, and thrust it into His riven side, *and be not faithless, but believing*[4]*!*

For every condition of man the Lord is at hand:

[1] Isai. lv. 6.   [2] Luke viii. 45.   [3] Luke vi. 46.
[4] Joh. xx. 27.

whosoever will, while yet his day of grace lasts, may draw nigh with his confessions and his supplications. *Not to judge the world, but to save the world*[1], the Lord is at hand.

But St Paul was not thinking of the first touch of all, when he thus wrote. He was speaking to those of whom he might hope that they already believed, already knew and already loved Christ. And are there not some such here also? some who are walking humbly with their God[2], and who, believing in Him, believe also in a Saviour[3]? some—many, we trust— who are about to kneel at His holy Table, penitent and believing, as guests whom He has bidden and *will in no wise cast out*[4]? Let these listen, with thankful hope, to the words now sent to them by the Lord of the feast, *I myself am near: be anxious about nothing, but in everything, by prayer and supplication, with thanksgiving, let your requests be made known unto God.*

Be anxious about nothing. It is a word of frequent recurrence in Scripture. *Take therefore no thought (be not anxious) for the morrow; for the morrow shall take thought (be anxious) for the things of itself*[5]. *When they deliver you up, take no thought (be not anxious) how or what ye shall speak: for it shall be given you in that same hour what ye shall speak*[6]

---

[1] Joh. xii 47
[2] Mic. vi. 8
[3] Joh. xiv. 1.
[4] Joh. vi. 37.
[5] Mat. vi. 34.
[6] Matt. x. 19.

Martha, Martha, thou art careful (anxious) and troubled about many things: but one thing is needful[1]. Even thus here. *Be anxious about nothing.*

Who does not feel the wisdom of this charge? What good can anxiety do? Anxiety, in itself, is an idle thing: the mind hovers and flutters round the subject, goes over the same ground again and again, wearies itself in vain repetitions of the same cares and fears. but what has it done? has it advanced the matter one real step? has it arrived at one good counsel, or set itself to one wise act? Anxiety is an enfeebling thing. it eats the very life out of the energies. it leaves the man not only where he was, but ten times less capable and less vigorous than at the beginning Anxiety is an irritating thing: it ruffles the temper, it upsets the balance of the spirit, it is the sure source of moodiness and sharpness and petulance and anger; it sets a man at war with himself, with his neighbour, with God's Providence and God's appointments Anxiety is a sign of mistrust, a sign of feeble faith, of flagging energy, and languid obedience

Yes, it is all this, and more: we know it, we confess it, we repent of it, and fall into it again. St Paul knew us better than to attempt the correction of anxiety by human arguments. It may be useless, it may be wrong, it may be mischievous. but it is in us

[1] Luke x. 41, 42.

all; and let a man be sharply tried, he is anxious still. The conflict with any one of our evil tendencies is too strong for us single-handed. Bring in another person; introduce a new consideration: suggest a new motive. Tell us, not that anxiety is wrong, not that it is injurious to ourselves, not that it is unprofitable to others, not that it is an ingratitude, not that it is a mistrust, not that it is an impiety; but tell us of One who amongst our other griefs has borne this, amongst our other sorrows has carried this[1]; tell us of One who in all our afflictions is Himself afflicted[2], in all our cares is Himself troubled; tell us, above all, of One who is not in some other, some different, some distant world, where the sound of human groans scarcely penetrates, where the burden of human distress is regarded as visionary or unreal, but who is here, in our world, at hand, near, present; who both foresees and remembers with us, feels with as well as for us, is *touched with the sense of our infirmities,* yea, was Himself *tempted in all points like as we are, yet without sin*[3]. Then, in His presence, in His human soul, in His compassionate heart, we will lay aside our anxieties, we will rest from our burdens, we will take refuge from our fears and from our sins.

But is there no place, some one asks, for anxiety? no room on any subject, for care, misgiving, and

[1] Isai. liii. 4. [2] Isai. lxiii. 9. [3] Heb. iv. 15.

apprehension? St Paul seems to leave none. *Be anxious about nothing...in everything let your requests be made known unto God.* And is not this human wisdom, as well as human happiness? Is your anxiety about circumstances? Are you afraid of coming to poverty? Is trade going against you? Do you see yourself outstripped by younger or busier rivals? Will anxiety avail anything against this form of evil? Will it not rather tend to paralyze than to stimulate exertion? Say to yourself rather *The Lord is at hand.* to Him I will go, with Him will I leave my burden. *the Lord will provide*[1] Or is your anxiety about the health of some one most dear to you? Do you see a daily decline of strength and spirits, of mind and life? The Lord is at hand: and He is the *Lord of life and death and of all things to them pertaining*[2]. To Him, by prayer and supplication, with thanksgiving, let your requests all be made known. Or is it the soul of some loved friend which is trembling in the balance? some unruly son, some worldly brother, or immoral husband? Hard indeed is it, most hard, in such a case, to apply the rule of the text. so hard to pray hopefully for one who has long *done despite unto the Spirit of grace*[3], so hard to pray without hope, and harder still to hope without prayer! And yet even here, even in this saddest and darkest of all trials, we have

[1] Gen xxii. 8   [2] Visitation Service   [3] Heb x 29

no other resource, and we believe that we need no other, than that which is here supplied to us; still, in everything, by prayer and supplication, with thanksgiving—may you not thank God that the door of grace, as of life, still stands open?—let your requests be made known unto God. Who can tell if He who does for us *exceeding abundantly above all that we ask or think*[1] may not do even this, and give to believing importunity a boon beyond calculation, beyond *the manner of man*[2], beyond human hope?

Wherefore lift up the hands which hang down, and strengthen the feeble knees[3]. We are not straitened in God: we are straitened in our own selves[4], our own faith, our own hope, our own prayer. We will draw nigh, yet once more, to our Lord Jesus Christ Himself, in that ordinance which He has instituted for our perpetual good and growth in grace; and prove Him now herewith, if He will not, in answer to earnest prayer, *open to us the very windows of heaven, and pour us out a blessing, that there shall not be room enough to receive it*[5]!

[1] Eph. iii. 20 [2] 2 Sam. vii. 19 [3] Heb. xii. 12
[4] 2 Cor. vi. 12 [5] Mal. iii. 10.

FIFTH SUNDAY IN LENT,
April 6, 1862.

LECTURE XIX.

PHILIPPIANS IV. 8, 9.

8   *FINALLY, brethren, whatsoever things are true, whatsoever things are venerable, whatsoever things are just, whatsoever things are pure, whatsoever things are lovely, whatsoever things are of good report, if there be any virtue and if there be any praise, these things take into your account.*

9   *The things which ye both learned, and received, and heard, and saw in me, these things practise: and the God of peace shall be with you.*

LECTURE XIX.

PHILIPPIANS IV. 8.

Finally, brethren, whatsoever things are true, whatsoever things are honest, whatsoever things are just, whatsoever things are pure, whatsoever things are lovely, whatsoever things are of good report, if there be any virtue, and if there be any praise, think on these things.

THE verse read as the text contains a direction for thought, the verse which follows it adds a direction for conduct and a promise conditional upon obedience to the two. *Think on these things...those things do... and the God of peace shall be with you.*

Our last subject was, Anxiety and its cure. *The Lord is at hand: be careful for nothing: but in everything, by prayer and supplication, with thanksgiving, let your requests be made known unto God. And the peace of God, which surpasseth every understanding—*which no human mind can of itself apprehend, and which no human mind enlightened from above will ever comprehend in its length and in its breadth—*shall guard your hearts and your thoughts in Christ Jesus.* If the Lord Jesus Christ is at hand, ready and willing to be approached and spoken to, if you are encouraged and commanded to make your desires on every subject known to One who hears and can help, then why should you be anxious? Avail yourself of the Lord's nearness, avail yourself of the permission to ask of God, and anxiety will be as needless as it is always useless So shall a peace not of earth but of heaven keep as in a fortress the heart and its thoughts. the seat of thought and the working of thought will both be safely kept where your true life itself is hidden, *with Christ in God*[1].

The text immediately follows.

Finally, brethren, for the rest, as that which completes and concludes all that has been said, *whatsoever things are true, whatsoever things are venerable,* worthy of respect and reverence, *whatsoever things are just, whatsoever things are pure, whatsoever things are lovely, whatsoever things are of good report, if there be any virtue and if there be any praise*—whatsoever is virtuous, and whatsoever is praiseworthy—*these things take into your account*[2], these things consider and reflect upon and meditate: let your thoughts be occupied with things true and grand and righteous

---

[1] Col iii. 3.   [2] *Verse* 8.

and pure, things lovely in themselves and of good report amongst good men, things virtuous in the sight of God and commended on earth by God's children. Let these things, and no others, be the topic of your thoughts, the subject of your meditations

The things which ye both learned, were taught when ye became Christians, as rules and principles of your new life, *and received* from me your Evangelist as transmitted to you from your new Master, *and heard* from my lips in preaching and in conversation, *and saw in me*, my life exemplifying what my doctrine prescribed, *these things practise*[1], let these things be your habit of life; live in all respects as I taught you, as I transmitted to you, as I bade you, as I myself shewed you and led the way.

And the God of peace shall be with you. Thus, and not otherwise, by so thinking and so doing, by following this twofold direction for thought and for conduct, thus and thus only shall you have with you Him whose chosen title is the God of peace His faithful servants not only have His favour and His blessing, they have Him also Himself with them, even as it is written, *I will dwell in them, and walk in them, and I will be their God, and they shall be my people*[2]. It is a serious question, therefore, Are we so thinking and so acting as to have the promise of God's living presence realized and fulfilled in ourselves?

[1] *Verse* 9   [2] 2 Cor vi. 16

Think on these things. Some persons say, I cannot help my thoughts. My mind will run on certain subjects: how can I control it? Sufferings which much affect me, injuries which have sunk into my soul, fears and dangers which stare me in the very face, how can I divert my thoughts from these pressing topics? And others say, In a world so full of excitements, at an age or under circumstances so powerfully influenced by pleasure, how is it to be expected that I should not look back and look forward to scenes of amusement and gaiety, to sights that charm and persons that attract me? And others say, In a world so wicked, so full of vice, so overflowing with crime, and with a mind naturally prone, as God made it, to inquisitiveness and curiosity, how can I avoid the presence of thoughts far from pure, far from virtuous, far from lovely or of good report? it is incident to my position in a world of evil, that vice rather than virtue should be presented to my mind and recalled to my memory. In short, disagreeing in much else, men are much alike in this, that they declare themselves unable to control thought, to coerce imagination, to curb memory, or to say to the mysterious being within each of them, Thus shalt thou think, thus shalt thou picture, thus shalt thou work and meditate, thus shalt thou forecast and recollect.

And yet St Paul seems to say that this which

flesh and blood cannot do is possible and necessary to the Christian. *Think on these things.* Take care —and therefore it must be in your power to take care —that your thoughts shall run on things right and good, beautiful and great, virtuous and praiseworthy.

And I well know that all who hear me have had experience, by contraries at least, of the importance of this rule. How many persons are made or kept frivolous chiefly by an inability to prescribe the subjects which their mind shall run upon ! They would give, or fancy they would give, all they possess, for the power to say decisively but for one half-hour or for one five minutes, This and not this shall be the subject of my thoughts. But they find that when they open the Bible the mind has flown away to some meditation of things present and transitory, when they kneel down to pray, even attention is absent, they cannot remember God's presence, much less can they wish the thing which they profess to pray for. Such persons are good judges of the importance of St Paul's precept, however little they may believe in the possibility of obeying it. For indeed it is a very dreadful thing, when we reflect upon it—a strong proof, were there no other, of our fallen and ruined state—that a man should thus sit at a helm of which he has lost the rudder, should thus be responsible for the conduct of a mind over which practically he has no control And if that responsibility cannot be denied, if *out of the heart the mouth speaketh*[1], if by the heart the path of life is chosen and the course of life shaped; in short, if (in every sense of the words) *out of the heart are the issues of life*[2], and according to the life must be the eternal judgment of each one of us[3]; how terrible must it be to be unable from a moral impotency to obey the charge, *Keep that heart with all diligence;* to be compelled to let thought drift whither it will, and yet to know that thought guides action, and action may destroy the soul!

We can all appreciate the importance of being able to control and guide our thoughts. We can all understand that it must be a serious thing to have lost or not to possess the power of doing so. And who has not known by experience something of the evil effects of thinking of the opposite things to those which St Paul here recommends? If there is one thing upon which all moralists are agreed, it is, the danger of bad company; the risk of living much with those who are either vicious or ungodly; the duty of taking heed to the choice of friends, and of allowing no other consideration to weigh with us in that choice in comparison with the question of the moral and religious character. It is not only, if chiefly, that we have to apprehend from an ill-chosen associate direct temptation or solicitation to sin. But it is that there is a damaging and deteriorating effect in the mere

[1] Matt. xii. 34 [2] Prov. iv 23. [3] 2 Cor v 10.

converse and contact of low morality and want of principle. Few men rise much above the level of the society in which they live hence, first, the responsibility of those who constitute that society one for another, hence, secondly, the duty of taking heed how we expose our own principles to a trial to which they may be unequal

But that which the society of other men does for us, for good or else for evil, in its influence upon our judgments and our actions, is done scarcely less by that sort of association which is entirely within the precincts of the mind itself, the association of thought; the things with which reflection busies itself, and which it entertains habitually as its companions and acquaintances within St Paul evidently felt that a Christian must take as much heed to this sort of familiarity as to the other, to the companionship with things as to the companionship with persons. He bids the Philippians to entertain one kind of guests within, and (by inference) to exclude or expel another And which of us does not feel that there is wisdom in this caution ? A man who lives much amongst the evil things of human nature, even if professional or other duty requires it of him, can seldom preserve unsullied the purity of his Christian feeling. The effect of a long life in the world is commonly, under any circumstances, somewhat injurious in this respect · if it tends to make a man more charitable, more tolerant of imperfections, more indulgent to the weaknesses and inconsistencies of human nature, it is apt also to render him less sensitive to sin, less keen in his abhorrence of ungodliness and vice, less able than at first to retain the accuracy of his Christian judgment and the elevation of his moral standard. How much more if he has been rather conversant with the evil than with the good parts of human character, if his work has lain chiefly among the wrongs and the crimes which fill our jails with felons, and make our homes miserable and desolate!

But if such be the effects of an acquaintance with things hateful and impure in those who approach them at the call of business and duty, how must it be with persons who live amongst them by choice? There are those who gloat upon the records of vice and crime, and find in them an attraction and a fascination which is wanting in things lovely and of good report. What an influence must be exerted on the whole through the length and breadth of the land, by those daily chronicles of ingenious villany or monstrous wickedness which a teeming press disseminates! Those annals of sin are the literature of half the nation. It is from them that whole classes take their notions of human nature and human life, their topics of common conversation, their materials for solitary reflection. Can we wonder if this constant handling and pondering of things not pure, not honest, not virtuous nor of good report, is found to lower the tone, to debase the imagination, and to corrupt the morality of those who practise it? if the touching of this pitch works defilement, and the familiarity with this vile example is followed too often by its imitation?

We all think meanly of a person whose chief pleasure is in reading the reports of police-courts, or frequenting as a mere pastime places where crime is tracked out, hunted down, and sentenced. And yet how many of us are guilty, less or more, of that which St Paul here by implication reproves! How many men, and women too, employ their precious time in reading fictitious narratives of no elevated or elevating character; narratives of which the best that can be hoped is that they may abstain from details of sin, that they may either content themselves with describing the follies of mankind, or if they touch upon vice, may at least show how it works out punishment, shame, and death! And how many more amongst us in their daily conversation delight to dwell not upon the virtues or merits but upon the faults and falls of their brethren! What visible pleasure is derived by many from the rumour of another's sin! How they repeat, embellish, and enlarge the story, till it has ceased altogether to present truth or fact! And all this oftentimes not though but because they themselves have similarly sinned and similarly suffered ; or because they bear in their bosom the hidden sting of an unsuspected transgression, and rejoice that the company of the sinful should grow and multiply before they themselves are openly added to it

Thus in divers ways and from various motives we are in danger, every one of us, of forgetting St Paul's warning to let our meditation be of things honest and pure, of things lovely and of good report The charge has a depth of wisdom and a wholesomeness of counsel scarcely noticed perhaps on its surface. It is a good thing that the subjects of our thoughts should be as much as possible good things and not evil Not only ought we resolutely to banish all wicked and sinful imaginations, all retrospects of evil deeds, all picturings of the pleasures of sin, all plannings and schemings of forbidden indulgences in the future . these are positive sins, and no Christian can be ignorant of their inherent sinfulness But St Paul tells us that we ought, as far as possible, to turn aside from the contemplation, from the recollection, of sins and faults not our own. We ought to cherish only such thoughts even concerning others, as are lovely and of good report We ought to dwell by choice only upon virtues. We ought to think good of others where we can, and where we cannot think good, there we ought at least to forget the evil. It does us harm to let our thoughts run upon it. It has a deteriorating and debasing effect upon ourselves. It is like living in bad company. It tends to make us first self-satisfied, and then careless, and then acquiescers in, and then imitators of evil. It habituates us to a bad atmosphere, and insensibly poisons the springs of life within. Things true, not deeds and words of falsehood; things honourable and venerable, things grand and majestic, not such as are mean and ignoble and contemptible; things just and righteous, not such as rob God of His honour and man of his right; things pure and chaste, not unclean and immoral; things lovely, not hateful; things of good report, not scandalous nor disgraceful; things virtuous, not vicious; things commendable, not blameworthy; these are the proper topics of a Christian's willing meditation. The great exploits and great characters of history; the noble works and self-denying sacrifices of charity; the manly vigorous exertions of public and private life; the lofty hopes and stirring interests of our country and our time; the great conceptions and glorious words of writers illustrious and immortal; above all, the disclosures of truth divine and eternal made to us in the inspired Word of Revelation; these are the things in which the mind and soul of man ought rather to expatiate: to have the heart preoccupied with these, to turn to them from petty, paltry, worthless trifles, from idle, scandalous, slanderous tales, from stories probably false and certainly mischievous, is a safeguard such as none can despise who either knows anything of *the plague of his own heart*[1], or of the festering sores which are eating everywhere into the body of our social life

My brethren, the charge given in the text presupposes a power over the thoughts Many, we have said, have not acquired or have lost that power. In the same way in which many have lost or have never cared to gain the control of their conduct, the power to say and to make it good, This will I do, and that will I not do, because this is right and because that is wrong; in the same manner, and for the same reason, many are destitute of the strength of will to think of this, and not to think of that, because this is salutary and profitable, and because that is injurious, enfeebling, or corrupting. And thus we are led to a serious concluding reflection upon the importance of turning our faith to account in the work of regulating and disciplining thought. Of ourselves we can neither think nor do one good thing. But if the Gospel be true, we can think as well as do all things through Christ who strengtheneth us[2]. Let us pray to God, as we have already prayed to-day, to *cleanse the thoughts of our hearts by the inspiration of His Holy Spirit*. Let us ask of God, as we

[1] 1 Kings viii 38.   [2] Phil. iv. 13.

have already asked to-day, mercifully to *grant that His Holy Spirit may in all things direct and rule our hearts*, through His Son our Lord Jesus Christ Let us begin, if we have never begun before, to practise ourselves in choosing and in refusing in the province of thought as well as of action. Let us learn from the Holy Spirit daily sought and hourly cherished, the power to invite and to exclude in the entertainment of guests in the house of the soul within. Let us go in quest of some thoughts, and let us bar and lock out others Few of us practise meditation Few of us devote even a brief moment or two of the day to the work of reflecting and meditating upon God and Christ, upon the word of Revelation, upon the condition of the soul, and the realities of eternity. Prayer, and that a poor brief hurried exercise, is the only religious duty with most of us. We do not preface it by meditation; we do not follow it by study ; we do not connect one stated season of prayer with another by patient deliberate resolute thoughts of good. Let the subject which has now engaged us teach a better lesson. More especially to the younger members of this congregation would we say with all seriousness and with all earnestness, Begin early, God being your helper, to be masters within. Begin early, God being your helper, to think as well as to do things true and honest, things just and pure, things lovely and of good report. Remember that the judgment of God will be a judgment upon thoughts as well as upon actions. When the Lord comes He will not only *bring every work into judgment*[1], but will *make manifest the counsels of the hearts*[2]. Only he whose heart is clean can depend upon keeping his life clean: and he only will have a clean heart, whose daily and hourly prayer from his youth up has been that of the inspired Psalmist, *Search me, O God, and know my heart; try me, and know my thoughts: and see if there be any wicked way in me, and lead me in the way everlasting*[3]

[1] Ecc. xii. 14. [2] 1 Cor iv 5. [3] Ps. cxxxix 23, 24.

First Sunday after Easter,
April 27, 1862.

LECTURE XX.

10   But *I rejoiced in the Lord greatly that now at length ye revived as to thinking for me; a matter of which ye*
11   *did also think, but had no opportunity. Not that I speak in respect of want, for I learned in the things in which*
12   *I am to be contented. I know both how to be abased, I know also how to abound, in everything and in all things I have been initiated both to be fully fed and to be hungry, both*
13   *to abound and to be in want. I am strong* [*to do*] *all*
14   *things in Him who enables me. But ye did well in having*
15   *partaken with my affliction. And ye also know, Philippians, that in the beginning of the Gospel, when I went out from Macedonia, no congregation imparted to me as to an*
16   *account of giving and receiving, but ye alone; for even in Thessalonica both once and twice ye sent to me for my need.*
17   *Not that I seek the gift; but I seek the fruit which redounds*
18   *as to an account of you. And I have to the full all things, and abound; I have been filled to the full, having received from Epaphroditus the things from you, an odour of a*
19   *sweet smell, a sacrifice acceptable, well-pleasing to God. And my God will fulfil every need of yours, according to His*
20   *riches in glory in Christ Jesus, and to God our Father be the glory unto the ages of the ages. Amen.*

21   Salute every saint in Christ Jesus. The brethren with
22   me salute you. All the saints salute you, and especially those of Cæsar's house.

23   The grace of the Lord Jesus Christ be with your spirit

LECTURE XX.

PHILIPPIANS IV. 13.

I can do all things through Christ which strengtheneth me.

WE approach the end of the Epistle which has been under our consideration for the last six months. God leave us not without His blessing! If any thoughts of good have been awakened in any of us by the study of this portion of His Word, may He enable us by His continual grace to bring those thoughts to good effect! And may He grant also that when in the remaining years of our pilgrimage we have recourse any of us to this book of Holy Scripture, whether in the order of daily reading, or under circumstances of anxiety, difficulty, or distress, we may find it more full of the needful instruction, guidance, and comfort, for our meditations upon it in the period which is now ending!

The course of the Apostle's communication turns

back, in these latest verses, to topics of a personal kind He has enforced upon his beloved readers the importance of concord, of union, of Christian love. He has taught them that a spirit of holy joy is not more a Christian's privilege, than it is a Christian's duty. He has struck at the root of that which interferes with and precludes joy, by reminding them that their Lord is always at hand to hear and to answer prayer, and that therefore all corroding care is as needless as it is fruitless. If anything makes you anxious, carry it to your Master, and so the peace of God will keep your hearts and your thoughts, whatever betides. He has added a special charge as to the government of the thoughts. Let your meditations be all upon things holy and wholesome, things lovely and of good report. So will your conduct also be Christian. You will do what my teaching enjoined, what my life exemplified: and the God of peace will be with you.

And now for a few parting words of personal gratitude for kindnesses received.

But I rejoiced in the Lord greatly that now at length ye revived as to thinking for me; a matter of which ye did also think, but had no opportunity[1].

The Christians at Philippi had lately sent some contributions to their beloved Apostle in his imprisonment at Rome[2]. When he was at large, he maintained himself by his own manual labour[3]: but now

[1] *Verse* 10.   [2] Acts xviii 3.   [3] Acts xx 34.

at Rome, with a soldier[1] chained night and day to his arm, this was impossible. He was thrown upon the support of God and of His Church, without the means, during two whole years, of doing anything for himself. And God, who cares for all who will cast their care upon Him[2], put it into the heart of that distant congregation at Philippi, to think of him in temporal things who had so thought of them in spiritual things[3]. That is the subject of the passage now before us. They had *revived*, he says, or, more exactly—for it is a figure taken from that beautiful burst of spring which we are now enjoying—they had, like a tree long bare and frost-bound, put forth new sprouts and shoots under the genial influence of God's rain and sunshine—they had thus sprouted and germinated afresh, after a season of apparent deadness, in their care or thought for him. But no sooner has he written the word *revived* or *put forth afresh* than he feels, with that quickness and delicacy of perception which is one of the great charms of St Paul's character as disclosed to us in his history and Epistles, that the expression may seem to involve a reproach for the lateness or tardiness of their offering; and therefore he adds instantly, that he knows that they had all along been thinking and caring for him, and had only wanted the opportunity of actually shewing and proving it.

[1] Acts xxviii. 16.   [2] 1 Pet. v. 7.   [3] 1 Cor. ix. 11.

For this, he says, he *rejoiced in the Lord* Their kindness had given him pleasure, not as a man only, but as a Christian. And he goes on to tell them why.

Not that I speak in respect of want: when I say that I rejoice in your gift, I do not say it in reference to deficiency or distress on my part; *for I learned*, when I became a Christian—learned (as the original language shews) as a single and final lesson—*in the things in which I am*, whatever circumstances I am in, *to be contented*[1]. The word is exactly *self-sufficing*, and so *independent*. Like our own word *contented*, which properly means *contained*, the opposite of one who is ever leaking or overflowing into something which is not his, even so the term here employed by St Paul denotes a man who, instead of hanging upon other things and other people, is sufficient, by God's grace, to himself, is satisfied to have what he has, much or little, and casts not a longing or a restless eye to that which God in His Providence has seen fit to deny to him. I learned in becoming a Christian, to be a self-sufficing, independent, contained and so contented man.

I know both how to be abased, brought to a low condition in outward things, *I know also how to abound: in everything and in all things I have been instructed* —the word is properly *initiated*, taught as a secret or

[1] *Verse* 11.

mystery communicated only to the selected few—*both to be fully fed and to be hungry, both to abound and to be in want*[1]. I have learned the Christian secret of universal contentment. Christ has taught me how to deal with abundance and with want, with circumstances of affluence and with circumstances of straitness. *I am strong* to do *all things*—the word *to do* is not in the original—*I have strength for all things in Him who enables me*[2]. A Christian is a man in Christ. In Him, as contained and included in Him, and therefore possessing His resources of grace and strength, even His own animating, strengthening, and upholding Spirit, *in Him who enables me I have strength for all things*, whether to do or to endure.

But, though Christ enables me to endure want when it comes to me, *ye did well in having partaken with*, shared, made common cause with, *my affliction*[3]. By sending help to me in my present distressed condition, you as it were made that condition your own; you took part in it, and so aided me in bearing it

And ye also know, Philippians, ye, as well as I, *that in the beginning of the Gospel*, in the early days of your discipleship, *when I went out from Macedonia*, when I went on from your country to others, *no congregation imparted to me as to an account of*, in regard to, *giving and receiving*, in the matter of contributing to my support by pecuniary or other gifts, *but ye*

[1] *Verse* 12.   [2] *Verse* 13   [3] *Verse* 14.

alone[1]. *For even in Thessalonica*[2], when I had but just left you, before I had even quitted the confines of Macedonia itself, *both once and twice*, not once only but twice over, *ye sent to me for my need*[3], ye sent to supply my want.

Not that I seek the gift[4]; do not suppose that in thus expressing myself I would have you imagine that it is the gift itself, the actual thing sent, that I desire: no, in this as in all else *I seek not yours but you*[5], and if I value the gift, it is because I see in it the givers. *Not that I seek the gift; but I seek the fruit which redounds* from such self-denying love *as to an account of you*, in regard to you. What I chiefly value in every such instance of your Christian thoughtfulness, is the assurance thus given me of your great and ever-growing reward in heaven. Nothing that a Christian does on earth for his Master or his brethren will fail to receive hereafter at that Master's hands a full recompence of reward.

And I have to the full all things, and abound. I desire that your love should bring after it for you a rich reward; and that desire is in the way to be accomplished. Your bounty towards me has been great indeed *I have been filled to the full*, my every want has been supplied, *having received from Epaphroditus the things from you, an odour of a sweet smell,*

[1] *Verse* 15 [2] Acts xvii 1. [3] *Verse* 16.
[4] *Verse* 17. [5] 2 Cor. xii. 14.

a sacrifice acceptable, well-pleasing to God[1]. The self-denying charity of the Philippians would rise to heaven like the scent of an acceptable sacrifice[2], bringing back God's blessing upon them. *And my God will fulfil every need of yours, according to His riches*, in the fulness of His own inexhaustible stores of good, *in glory*, in the manifestation of His excellency, by shewing forth what He Himself is in power and in goodness, *in Christ Jesus*[3], in whom He does all His acts, and most of all those acts which concern His redeemed people. *And to God our Father be the glory unto the ages of the ages. Amen*[4]. Praise be to Him for all His gifts! *Not unto us, O Lord, not unto us, but unto Thy name give the praise, for Thy loving mercy and for Thy truth's sake*[5]*!*

Salute every saint, every individual Christian amongst you, *in Christ Jesus*, in the exercise of that brotherhood which subsists among us all in virtue of our several and separate union with and incorporation in Christ. *The brethren with me salute you*[6]. *All the saints salute you, and especially those of Cæsar's house*[7], those members of the Emperor's household, whether bond or free, whom St Paul's imprisonment had been the means, directly or indirectly, of bringing to faith in Christ.

[1] *Verse* 18. [2] Gen. viii. **20**, 21. [3] *Verse* 19.
[4] *Verse* 20. [5] Ps. cxv 1. P. B. [6] *Verse* 21.
[7] *Verse* 22.

The grace, the favour and blessing, *of the Lord Jesus Christ be with your spirit*[1].

There are many topics, my brethren, which might engage our attention in this closing passage of the Epistle. But none surely can be so wide in its interest or so close in its application—none, certainly, so appropriate to that solemn act of Communion which is to complete our present service—as that which the words of the text itself suggest: *I can do all things,* or *I am strong for all things, in Him who enables me, in Christ who strengtheneth me.*

The context shews that it is more of bearing than of doing that St Paul here speaks. He has been initiated, he says, in the great mystery of contentment. He has learned of his Master, in whatever circumstances he is, therein to be self-sufficing, therewith to be content. He knows how to reconcile himself to every extreme; how to conduct himself in plenty and in hunger, in abundance and in need. *I can do all things through Christ who strengtheneth me.* The last words both give the secret of the former, explain the spring and source of the contentment spoken of, and are also by the former, not circumscribed or limited, but at least pointed and applied. It is true in every sense of a Christian, certainly it was true in every sense of St Paul, that he can do all things through Christ strengthening him: but here

[1] *Verse* 23

we are especially called to notice that Christ enabled St Paul, and can enable all who believe, to be contented with any condition and with any circumstances of life which the Providence of God has been pleased to ordain.

We have seen already in some degree what contentment is. It is the being wholly contained within that space to which we are limited. It is the ready acquiescence of the heart and will in that which is, and is for us. It is the not reaching forth to that which is forbidden or denied to us. It is the not looking with eager desire through the bars of our cage at a fancied liberty or an imagined paradise without. It is the saying, and saying because we feel, in the deep of our soul, This is God's will, and therefore it is my will. It is the having God's will for our will in all things. That is contentment

The other word for the same virtue expresses the same result in a different form. It calls it, as St Paul here calls it, a spirit and a state of *self-sufficing*. That is, the not hanging upon some thing or some person out of myself for my happiness; the not depending for tranquillity or for repose or for comfort upon outward circumstances which I cannot control, or upon other human beings whose feelings and actions I cannot command. It is the condition of one who is independent of all save God, of one whom neither riches nor poverty, neither affluence nor want, neither success nor failure, neither prosperity nor adversity, can so affect as to make the difference to him of being a happy man or a miserable.

Certainly we can all exclaim with St Paul in another of his Epistles, If this be so, *godliness with contentment is great gain*[1]*!* This spirit must be a desirable one, could we but attain it. To be independent of outward things, to be independent of other persons, what a boon, what a privilege, what an elevation!

How rare, my brethren, amongst men is a true spirit of contentment! Even in prosperity how rare is it! We sometimes say that it is rarer in prosperity than even in adversity. There have been more marked and notorious cases of discontent in high positions and great fortunes than in humbler and less enviable conditions of life. It may be, chiefly, that they are more striking: there is a sharpness of contrast between the outward and the inward condition, there is a sadness and a bitterness in the thought of great blessings unthankfully and despitefully used, which makes the case of a discontented prosperity more noticeable than that of a peevish and irritable adversity. But when we extend the range of observation and enter more seriously into the reasons, we shall perceive that there is more in it than this. A condition of prosperity has a direct tendency to relax

[1] 1 Tim. vi. 6.

the sinews of the self-command within, and to make the whole moral frame languid, flaccid, and feeble. In that condition every little hindrance to perfect self-indulgence (and whose life does not present some such hindrances?) is regarded as a serious calamity; too often as an injury received, and an injury to be resented. Hence the prosperous man is oftentimes found not only living without God, but fighting against God in His Providence and in His grace.

It is needless to apply the same remark to circumstances of a generally adverse kind. No wonder those whose life is a daily dying—a daily thwarting of the will, a daily privation of the comforts and almost of the necessaries of existence, or a daily stretching of the body on a rack of sharp and bitter pain—find it difficult to say, This condition contents me, I look not out of it, I am independent of circumstances, I find my inner personal being self-sufficing still! Blessed be God, there are those who can say this. But it is not of nature that they learned the lesson. No mere evenness of natural temper, and no mere insensibility of natural feeling, can really simulate, successfully, consistently, and permanently, the grace which beamed forth from an Apostle's life when he wrote from his custody in the tyrant city, *I am strong for all things in Him who enables me.*

Such contentment is, as he himself here writes, of the nature of a secret or mystery communicated only by special revelation to a selected few. *I have been initiated*, he writes, in it. My brethren, who tells that secret? who initiates in that Divine mystery? It must be a Person. We do not hear secrets from the whispering winds: we are not initiated in mysteries by common rumour or by the passing changes and chances of mortal life. I learned that lesson, St Paul says in effect, from Him who once arrested me by His own authoritative voice in the midst of a campaign against His cause and His people, and who from that day to this has had me in His holy keeping, under His wise instruction, His loving counsel, His needful and salutary discipline. His Holy Spirit abiding within me, *setting me free* by His own presence *from the law of sin and death*[1], correcting me when I err, recalling me when I wander, raising me when I stumble, yea, abiding within me as the very life of my life and soul of my soul, has taught me, is teaching me still, that whatever is is right, that what God wills ought to be my will, and that all things, even the most painful and the most adverse, are ever *working together for good to them that love Him*[2]. Thus that contentment which in one sense is a mystery is in an equally true sense a grace and a strength. And if they who acquire it are few, few in comparison with the multitudes who prefer guiding their own life and think themselves perfectly able to

[1] Rom. viii. 2.   [2] Rom. viii. 28.

dispense with God, yet is that not of the will of Him who *will have all men to be saved*[1], but only of that self-will which refuses to submit itself, even for salvation's sake, to the guidance of the All-wise, the Almighty, and the All-merciful *Ye will not come to me, that ye might have life*[2].

God save us all, beloved brethren, from that suicidal folly; the folly of those for whom Christ has done and is willing to do all things, but who will not be helped, will not be comforted, will not be blessed and saved! of those for whom God has spread here *a table in the wilderness*[3], but who will not *eat of His bread nor drink of the wine which He has mingled*[4]. We shall repent it one day! May it be before it is quite too late *to see one of the days of the Son of man*[5]; before *the things which belong to our peace are hidden* for ever *from our eyes*[6].

[1] 1 Tim. ii. 4. [2] John v 40 [3] Ps lxxviii 19.
[4] Prov. ix 5. [5] Luke xvii 22 [6] Luke xix. 42.

SECOND SUNDAY AFTER EASTER,
May 4, 1862.

LECTURE XXI.

[This Lecture, though supplementary in its character, is added to the foregoing, as suggesting some practical considerations which may form no unfitting close to the course and to the Volume.]

LECTURE XXI.[1]

PHILIPPIANS IV. 17.

I desire fruit that may abound to your account.

WHERE is the Christian minister, from whose heart this cry has not risen?

The word *fruit* is of large significance. What a place it occupies in Nature! Where is the work of husbandry, or the process of animal or vegetable life, in which this is not the one point of importance, What fruit is there? *The husbandman waiteth for the precious fruit of the earth, and hath long patience for it*[2]. What if it comes not? What if after all his waiting, what if after all his toil, every blossom is cut off by frost, and every ear of corn spoilt by blight or mildew? Will he be consoled by the reflection that the trees in earlier spring were bright with every form

[1] A Collection was made on this occasion for the Church Missionary Society.

[2] James v. 7.

of promise, or that the fields were once green with the springing blade, wet with abundant rain, or warm with glorious sunshine? The one thing for which he looked was fruit. All else was valuable only as a prognostication of fruit. If the hope was not realized, it was rather a mockery than a satisfaction.

And this word *fruit* was transferred by the Gospel to other and yet more important uses. Trace it through the Scriptures of the New Testament, through the discourses of our Lord and through the writings of His Apostles, and how grave, how anxious, are the questions which it suggests to us for self-examination! *Bring forth therefore fruits worthy of repentance. Every tree which bringeth not forth good fruit is hewn down and cast into the fire*[1]. *By their fruits ye shall know them*[2]. *Let no fruit grow on thee henceforward for ever. The kingdom of God shall be taken from you, and given unto a nation bringing forth the fruits thereof*[3]. *Behold, these three years I come seeking fruit on this fig-tree, and find none: cut it down; why cumbereth it the ground*[4]? *Every branch in me that beareth not fruit, He taketh away: and every branch that beareth fruit, He purgeth it that it may bring forth more fruit*[5]. *But now, being made free from sin, and become servants to God, ye have your fruit unto holiness, and the end everlasting life*[6]. *The wisdom that is from*

---

[1] Luke iii 8, 9. [2] Matt. vii. 20. [3] Matt. xxi. 19, 43.
[4] Luke xiii. 7. [5] John xv. 2. [6] Rom. vi. 22.

above...is full of mercy and good fruits[1]. *Being filled with the fruits of righteousness, which are by Jesus Christ to the glory and praise of God*[2]. You see what God looks for; what is the one important question as concerns each of us; What fruit is there? In the great Parable[3] in which our Lord classified the hearers of His Gospel in all ages, the one distinction between false and true profession is made to be this; not so much, Did a man listen? not so much, Did a man receive? not so much, Did a man love the sound and entertain the demands of the Gospel? but rather, Was there any fruit? The three evil hearers were alike in this—by this they were all equally distinguishable from the good hearer—they brought no fruit to perfection; while he, in various degrees, but in reality, deed, and truth, was seen to produce fruit, to have a harvest, and that harvest solid, valuable, and abiding.

Well therefore may a Christian minister who understands the business of his high calling try himself and his ministry by this one criterion, Is there any fruit? Well may he, as he stands before his people in the exercise of his important and responsible ministry, address himself to them with all the earnestness of one pleading for his life, and say, *I desire fruit that may abound to your account.*

He will not indeed mislead them, or suffer them to mislead themselves, as to the nature of that fruit

[1] James iii. 17.   [2] Phil. i. 11.   [3] Matt. xiii. 3—23.

for which he looks. He will never speak of it as though a few isolated acts of self-denial or charity were infallible marks of good or certain prognostications of an eternal recompence. He will constantly remind them that only a heart right with God, only a heart truly repentant and truly believing, can originate such acts as God will recognize or approve. But on the other hand, marking well the signs of his times, and observing how widely diffused has now become, thanks be to God, the knowledge of the Gospel of faith and grace; how generally it is understood by professed Christians that merit is excluded, and that a doctrine of self-justifying works is a delusion and a mockery to sinful men; he will be keenly alive to an opposite and no less fatal danger, the danger of men's resting in supposed mental processes, in correct evangelical opinions, and feelings quickened into spiritual activity, without attending sufficiently to the state of the life, to the government of thought and speech, the predominance of devout affections, and the energy of a self-denying charity.

In this sense, my beloved brethren, I would earnestly ponder with you this morning the affectionate solicitude which breathes in the words of St Paul here addressed to the Philippians, *I desire fruit that may abound to your account.*

I will mention a few particulars which press themselves most urgently upon my attention.

It is now more than a year and a half since our relation towards each other as minister and congregation was first happily established. During that time there has been much for which I must ever feel thankful. Not only much kindness and courtesy, much personal goodwill expressed and reciprocated, many cases in which mutual regard has ripened into sincere friendship: but also (as I humbly hope) unmistakable proofs here and there of a lively interest in the higher purposes for which the Christian ministry was established, attention readily given to truths here enforced, and a response to opportunities of instruction considerably multiplied; and, let us not doubt but earnestly believe, cases in which the Spirit of God has carried home to the heart truths once neglected or despised, and made real to the soul matters which were before looked upon as mystical, visionary, or fanciful. No toil or exertion on man's part would have been wasted if but one such instance could be relied upon. The salvation of one soul would be a reward far beyond anything which human labour could have spent upon it.

But these results are among *the secret things* which *belong unto the Lord our God*[1]. When they are granted, they are granted most often in secret: it is not the faith which displays itself which is the most real or the most effectual. We must look also

[1] Deut. xxix. 29.

at the congregation. We cannot forget that every one of your souls is equally valuable and equally in danger. We cannot and we ought not to rest satisfied with the hope that here and there one or two are saved as brands from the burning[1]; we cannot reflect with satisfaction on a state of things in which the rule is indifference or inconsistency, and only the exception thoughtfulness, change, and salvation. When we say from this Pulpit, *I desire fruit that may abound to your account*, we never can forget that St Paul hoped the very best things for every one of his converts, hoped that of all his Philippian congregation not one soul might perish; we cannot acquiesce in a condition so fearfully inverted as that one or two amongst us might be saved and all but a few must perish. God forbid! May He of His infinite mercy so work betimes in the hearts of this people, that multitudes amongst us may find mercy in the day of His appearing[2]!

And now therefore let me suggest a few of those things which we ought to mean, for ourselves and for others, when we say, *I desire to see fruit.* Is it not, in other words, to say, I desire to see something come of our ministry amongst you? Fruit is produce. We know how terrible it would be for a husbandman to be sowing his seed year by year, and year after year to find that nothing resulted from it; that nothing

[1] Amos iv. 11; Zech. iii. 2.   [2] 2 Tim. i. 18.

came up, or nothing grew, or nothing ripened, or nothing was at last reaped and gathered. Do we suppose that he would acquiesce in all this? Do we imagine that he would have the heart to go on thus? Would he not begin to suspect either his seed or his ground? either his own care or the assiduity of his labourers? Such a state of things would soon be ended, either by his ceasing to sow, or by his beginning to reap. And why should it be altogether otherwise with us? Does it really make all the difference, that in our case we are dealing with spiritual things, and that in his case the seed and the harvest are alike natural and material? If the Word of God is true, our seed is just as real as his, and our harvest ten thousand times more important. It is true we cannot control the influences which counteract or give effect to our sowing. We have no power ourselves over your hearts; over the attention, over the reception, or over the things done in consequence of that attention and of that reception. These matters lie beyond our reach. But there is 'One who can control even these things[1]. And if He bade us sow, and if the seed is His, and if He is interested in the sowing, and if He has promised that in due season and in due measure *we shall reap if we faint not*[2], surely there must be something wrong in us (how can we judge otherwise?) if the return is scanty or

[1] 1 Cor. iii. 6.   [2] Gal. vi. 9.

none: surely, if you care for us, you ought even for our sake to aid us with your sympathy and with your prayers; you ought, above all, to aid us by submitting your own hearts earnestly to the sweet influences of God's Spirit; you ought to make these services as full and as devout and as successful as possible; you ought to crowd the house of God week by week with serious worshippers; you ought to flock to the Lord's Table when it is spread, to seek a double and a tenfold blessing upon yourselves, upon us, upon the congregation, upon the Church of Christ.

Knowing as we do God's faithfulness, we should regard it almost as fruit at once if we saw you intent upon seizing every opportunity of worship. We are so sure that God is *always more ready to hear than we to pray*, that if we saw you earnest in prayer and in the use of the means of grace, we should be equally certain that it was not in vain. But you know how our Lord Jesus Christ Himself was impeded when He was upon earth by human coldness and indifference. *He could there do no mighty work, save that He laid His hands upon a few sick folk, and healed them: and He marvelled because of their unbelief*[1]. It is so still. When He comes into a half-empty Church, or, still worse, into a Church frequented by careless and heartless worshippers; when He sees them not

[1] Mark vi. 5, 6.

caring to kneel, not thinking it worth while to respond in the supplications, or to sing His praise; when He sees them hastening away when His Table is prepared for His own heavenly feast, as though the rite were one either repulsive or contemptible: alas! my brethren, what can He do? I ask the question sadly, and I would ask it of you earnestly, What can the Lord Jesus Christ Himself do for such a congregation? Do not you perceive how His Divine hand, outstretched to heal and to save, is cramped and fettered by such unwillingness to receive? Do not you perceive that in order to His blessing us as He would there must be faith, there must be desire, there must be prayer, on the part of the human recipients? and then see if the words of the Prophet will not be again and again verified, *Behold, the Lord's hand is not shortened that it cannot save, neither His ear heavy that it cannot hear*[1]!

And then let us think also of the congregation when it has dispersed itself again. Let us see what the words *I desire fruit* will mean then; what they will mean in your hearts and in your homes.

The fruit of the Spirit is love, joy, peace, longsuffering, gentleness, goodness, faith, meekness, temperance[2]. O my brethren, how stands it with you as to fruits like these? Look at the character of the fruit

[1] Isai lix 1.   [2] Gal v. 22, 23.

which Christ seeks in you. Does not the very sound of the words breathe peace? O how different are these from the fruits of the natural heart, its anger and strife and contention, its self-seeking and self-pleasing, its resentments and ambitions and carnal lusts! *Love, joy, peace,* as though to reprove our tumults and bickerings and dissensions: *longsuffering, gentleness, goodness,* as though to say to us, *Take my yoke upon you and learn of me*[1]*; let this mind be in you, which was also in Christ Jesus*[2]*: faith, meekness, temperance,* as though to say to us, This is the Christian victory[3], over the world of sense, the devil of pride, and the self of flesh; this is he that overcometh evil, even he who through faith in Jesus Christ overcomes inclination, overcomes passion, overcomes sloth and self. My brethren, I would ask again, Which of you understands and feels that this, this only, is the fruit which God accepts? He who bears not this fruit, this fruit of the Holy Spirit, shewn in gentleness, shewn in quietness, shewn in self-command, shewn in faith and love, is a barren tree, a ground *bearing thorns and briars, rejected, nigh unto cursing, whose end is to be burned*[4]. O put aside, in Christ's name, in Christ's strength, all anger and malice and wrath and unkindness and boasting; *look not every one on his own things, but every one also on*

[1] Matt. xi. 29. [2] Phil. ii. 5. [3] 1 John v. 4.
[4] Heb. vi. 8.

the things of others; yea, I say it again, *let this mind be in* each of *you, which was also in Christ Jesus*[1]. Then shall we say, then shall One greater than we say also, I have found fruit on this tree; the fruit which I seek; the fruit which abides unto life eternal[2]!

To-day the desire for fruit has a special meaning. You are asked to-day, as individuals and as a congregation, to do something towards making the Gospel of Christ known to other nations. Now, my brethren, this call might be urged by various considerations. We might speak of the want which exists, and by reason of which millions of our race are perishing for lack of knowledge[3]. We might urge you by motives of humanity to give freely to others that greatest gift of all, which you yourselves have freely received[4]. Or we might address you as disciples of a Master who laid this solemn charge upon His servants, that they should *go into all the world and preach the Gospel to every creature*[5], and who appended to that charge, as though the two things went together, the blessed and comforting promise, *Lo, I am with you alway, even unto the end of the world*[6]. If you disobey the command to *go and teach all nations*, neither can you claim the promise, *Lo, I am with you alway.*

[1] Phil. ii. 4, 5. [2] John iv. 36. [3] Hos. iv. 6
[4] Matt. x. 8. [5] Mark xvi. 15. [6] Matt. xxviii. 20.

But I purpose this morning to confine myself to a single thought, that suggested in the text, *I desire fruit that may abound to your account.* It is true, your offerings are needed; they have a value of their own; God has assigned to this poor material thing which we call money an extraordinary position, a marvellous efficacy, in doing His work even for the souls of men. Money can create the machinery of missions. Without money we cannot even find the men. Without money the Gospel itself can scarcely *have free course and be glorified*[1]. Therefore let no man affect to despise it, or even to say, I care not whether your offerings of this kind be large or small, I think only of the giver, not of the gift. I cannot say so. I should be glad to see your contributions to-day large to overflowing. I should say, if I could think that any had given from an imperfect or faulty motive, *Notwithstanding, every way*, by this means *Christ is preached; and I therein do rejoice, yea, and will rejoice*[2]. But far more earnestly would I say, as the minister of this congregation, The chief thing which I desire is not the gift, but *I desire fruit that may abound to your account.*

In a certain sense all almsgiving abounds to the account of the giver. All almsgiving, I mean, which is worthy of the name. I may be glad of the gift given; but I cannot call it almsgiving of a Christian

---

[1] 2 Thess. iii. 1.   [2] Phil. i. 18.

kind unless there be two things in it—disinterestedness and self-denial. We must have no side-aims, no crooked or selfish motives, in that almsgiving which is to inherit the promise. A person must not give to be seen of men[1]. And a person must not give because not to give would be to be blamed by men. And a person must not give thus much, because to give less would appear mean or illiberal. These are bad motives; and half the almsgiving of Christian congregations is no doubt spoiled by them for the giver. Again, I cannot call it almsgiving in a high or Christian sense unless there is in it something of self-denial. I say again, it may do good without this; but it can bring no blessing after it. It is well from early years to associate the idea of giving to another with sparing from oneself. Let the little sum which you had intended to lay out upon self, in body or mind, be willingly and cheerfully given to another; to the relief of the body, the instruction of the mind, or the enlightenment of the soul, of some other person or persons, for whom, as for you, Christ died. Then that is Christian almsgiving: it is the act of one who out of love to Christ gives away that which he would have had to spend. Now all such almsgiving brings after it fruit which abounds to the giver. It brings after it God's blessing, God's approval, yes, let none pretend to be above the motive—the Scriptures are

[1] Matt. vi. 1.

full of it in the plainest and broadest terms—God's recompence of reward.

But most of all surely will this be so in cases where the act itself is an act of faith. To relieve distress, disease, destitution, when it stares you in the face, is better than not to relieve it; but it is oftentimes an act rather of natural kindness than of spiritual principle. But when you give with disinterestedness and self-denial in the cause of a Christian Mission, you are doing that which can be prompted by no such motive. Not only is the want which you seek thus to relieve a distant and an unseen want; not only is the object of your bounty unknown, and his country and race remote and different from yours; but also, if you saw him, the want would be only intelligible to the mind of a Christian, only visible to the eye of faith; your perception of its existence would prove you to have something of the Christian's estimate of things that are excellent, something of the mind of Christ Himself as to things important and desirable and true. And it is the certain reaction of such almsgiving, such in motive and such in object, that it strengthens the faith out of which it springs. A man, or a child, who has denied himself something that he may give to the cause of the Gospel and to the life of souls, cannot but find the sinews of his own faith braced by that exercise. He is reminded of his own great privileges, high hopes, and solemn responsibilities. *Unto whomsoever much is given*—such is the cry which echoes in his ears—*of him shall be much required*[1]. He is strengthened to remember this, to confess it, and to act upon it. And that congregation which gives largely in the cause of the evangelization of the nations, is evermore found to be a vigorous and thriving congregation. *He that watereth shall be watered also himself. There is that scattereth, and yet increaseth*[2]. The more widely you extend the circle of your sympathies in things spiritual, the more intensely do they act within that widened and widening circumference. The congregation which cares only for its own poor, its own sick, and its own schools, is ever a niggardly congregation even towards these. The congregation which opens its hand and spreads wide its sowing, regardless whether the claim is local or national or even world-wide, has always enough and to spare for its home charities, and it cares for them nobly. If then I desire fruit that may abound, beloved brethren, to your account, I ask you to give, as this day, liberally, and not to grudge. I ask you to rise out of the narrow limits of your town and neighbourhood, to let your charity and your humanity take a wider range and a loftier flight, and to give this day to your Master Himself, that He may be better known, that He may be more greatly honoured, *that His way may be known upon earth, His saving*

[1] Luke xii. 48. [2] Prov. xi. 24, 25.

health among all nations. Give in this spirit, give and spare not: and be assured that, so giving, *God, even your own God,* will largely *grant you His blessing*[1].

[1] Ps. lxvii. 2, 6.

FOURTH SUNDAY AFTER EASTER,
    May 18, 1862.

THE END.

www.ingramcontent.com/pod-product-compliance
Lightning Source LLC
Chambersburg PA
CBHW071227230426
43668CB00011B/1342